THEOLOGY
OF
WONDER

—

Bishop Seraphim Sigrist

OAKWOOD PUBLICATIONS
TORRANCE, CALIFORNIA

Cover copy: John McMahon
Cover painting: *Airscape 93113* by The Monks of New Skete
Typesetting and design by Studio 185

ISBN: 1-891295-17-9

Published by
    Oakwood Publications
    3827 Bluff St.
    Torrance CA 90505-6359

Dedicated to my brothers and sisters of Hosanna.

CONTENTS

PREFACE

Occasionally a book is given to us that helps us to see: to behold what was ever present yet obscured by sin, anxiety or pettiness. This is such a book. It is a poem in prose that describes in precious vignettes what only the mystics know intuitively, 'that everything is Gift.'

The author, a bishop of the Orthodox Church, leads the reader with him on a pilgrimage, a personal, inward journey, from below to above, from earth to heaven. Whether the rung on this mystical ladder concerns silence or holy folly, deification or community, it conveys treasures of wisdom and insight that require slow, meditative and repeated reading.

This Theology of Wonder is wonderful theology, offering as it does a rare, inspired glimpse into the simple things of daily life. Things that reveal and make accessible to us the presence, the love, and the ineffable beauty of God—but also of ourselves, as bearers of His image.

FR. JOHN BRECK
PROFESSOR OF NEW TESTAMENT
ST. SERGIUS, PARIS

FOREWORD

Over the centuries Christian theologians have devised widely divergent patterns or diagrams for the presentation of their materials. Some are clearly identifiable as to time and place. Bishop Seraphim here presents the Theology of Wonder ordered after a pattern which has distinct and helpful characteristics. He does not follow an easy-to-label format of systematic or dogmatic theology. He is contemporary without being trendy or postmodernistic. His categories have been around for ages and have a commanding vitality of their own. In some ways his approach suggests that of Charles Williams and the diagram of glory. And we are grateful for his calling upon Max Picard's *World of Silence*.

This is fresh and readily accessed mystical theology. Not a simple task at all, and yet presented with simplicity and singularity of intent. We come here to a clearing in the forest with no hut in sight.

It is a happy circumstance for those of us at Drew University that part of the core of this book was first delivered as a course on the Theology of Wonder which Bishop Seraphim taught in our Graduate School. I salute its publication with gratitude.

JAMES H. PAIN
DEAN OF GRADUATE SCHOOL
DREW UNIVERSITY

First Sound

By the road through Semhoz, a tiny Russian village, is a plain wooden marker at the spot where a modern saint, Father Alexander Men, was struck down by an assassin.

A pilgrim stops for a moment, touches the wood and signs the cross, and then crosses the road into the forest. For some way he follows a faint and intermittent path. It is an amazing day, the sky blue beyond blue, the colors of the flowers yellow and white; water runs along the path (though it is June) like water from melting snow; there is a very strong wind, but no harm from it, and the forest, all green, stretches away and away. The pilgrim begins to sing, "Alleluia..."

As he sings he is struck by a kind of awareness that perhaps the meaning, the depth, of that whole word cannot be accessible to him, but that the beginning of it, the sound 'A' is given him to know and express. He continues to sing, weeping uncontrollably for joy for twenty minutes as he walks a little further and then back to the road. A part of his mind continues to think, like an occasional teacher of obscure courses to

1

graduate students, then the syllable 'A' is of great significance to the Shingon school of Buddhism. But even this work of reflection, which normally is so able to filter out direct experience, does not stem the joy of that moment, that time of color and light and wind, a time seeming outside of the natural order, a time of Wonder.

St. Isaac of Syria speaks often of 'Wonder.' We should, he says, read the Bible "enveloped in Wonder," and "integrated knowledge is Wonder in God...this is the way to come in the freedom of immortal life."

The reflections that follow are attempts to sound and express the 'A' of Wonder in God, to whose Glory they are dedicated, and after that in love and devotion to the small community known as Hosanna which was meeting that day in a house to which the pilgrim now, and ever again, makes his way through the forest.

1

BERESHITH

BERESHITH. In the beginning. As we move back to the beginning, time takes on a different pace. Immeasurably more is within a primal instant than in a later year, and words must change too, to keep up, and science and myth find a single language in that time before their division.

Bereshith. That heart of light which is called now the 'Big Bang,' was understood by the medieval Robert Grosseteste who observed (in *De Luce*) that, given the nature of light to diffuse to a limit, we should regard the entire Cosmos as having been projected from a single point of light which, in its projection, becomes the world as we observe it.

St. Basil (in his treatise on the *Six Days of Creation*) writes,

> So the Divine Word made every object beautiful (by light) just as when men, in deep sea, pour in oil and make the surface around them clear.

Bereshith. Several of us from the seminary go to a class held late at night at a New York synagogue by Dovid Din, a rabbi and teacher. Our guide is named Al Nur, which means 'light.'

It is already eleven when Dovid enters the room. He is a striking figure, tall and very gaunt, in the black suit and broad-brimmed hat of a Hassid. By some trick of the reflection between my glasses and the lamps, his face vanishes for a moment in a blur of light.

Bereshith. "Now I will say something that is rather profound, if you are taking notes, write it down: this is important. With God the act of Creating and the act of sustaining are a single act. If you or I build a table, we first think how we will make it, and then we make it, and afterwards dust and polish it. But with God it is one single action."

This means that every day is the first day of creation because creation is a gift continually arriving and opening out... Is this not what St. Basil sees when he writes with such obvious delight,

> The meadows covered with deep grass, the fertile plains quivering with harvests and the movement of corn like the waves of the sea.
>
> HEXAMERON 5:6

And concerning the migration of fish,

> I myself have seen these marvels! And admired the wisdom of God in all things.

When St. Basil looks out from his home at Annesi, it is with the same eye of delight:

> There is a high mountain, very thickly wooded, watered from the north with cool and transparent

streams...Behind my home there is another valley rising into a ledge up above which gives a view of the extent of the plains which is no less beautiful...it is a most pleasant scene! The exhalations of the earth...the breezes from the river, the multitude of flowers, the singing birds...

LETTER 14

It is the eye of St. Francis looking out over the fertile plains of Umbria—the eye of a child—seeing each day as the First Day. The special green of early spring not fading, to that eye, but ever renewed. To see this is to see with the mind of a beginner, "not as having attained," St. Paul will say... Meeting God's beginning with one's own. Bereshith. Dovid says, "Those who pray see that the entire Universe is the breathing of God, and they breathe their prayer into that breath."

Bereshith. On the Seventh Day God rested, or rather, created rest. Fr. Alexander Schmemann would say that without the Holy Spirit, all things else, the dogmas and structures of the Church in history included, are but heaviness and oppression, but with the Spirit it lives. Is it no also so with Creation, that the Rest which God made on the Seventh Day brings the whole Universe to life? Rest is the soul of the body of the world.

And that creation of Rest opens out yet again, as St. Iranaeus says, to an Eighth Day which is beyond the week, beyond our experience of time. The day after Saturday, the seventh day, is the Eighth Day, the Day of Resurrection, the day of rest completed as the first day of a new time.

Bereshith. On the eve of the seventh day, some years later, as we experience our days' sequence, and a year after Reb Dovid's sudden death, Sister Tamara lights the candles for Sabbath in a house of the Beatitudes. For it is the custom of that Christian community today to keep also the first day of Rest. There is a clean white cloth on the table, and in the center a Cross.

Bereshith.

> Leka Dodi lekras kalo!
> Pnay Shabos nkablo!
> Come to my beloved to greet the bride!
> The Sabbath presence let us welcome!

Bereshith. A bearded man with a violin catches up the music and the dance begins around the table and then out through the halls...Some here were born Christian, and some were born to families where the candles were lit every seventh night, but the dance is one. It is said that to those of this dance, on this day, an extra soul descends... Could this which I feel be the soul of Dovid moving into, and calling us into a reconciliation beyond all expectation? And into a beginning?

BERESHITH.

2

Tree

THE WORLD'S FIRST COMPUTER was perhaps a tree—or rather a veritable grove of diagrams of trees, each branch and each leaf bearing a significance and place, in the art of Raimundo Lull, that myriad-minded twelfth-century Majorcan genius, who also may be credited, in Blaquerna, with the first real novel.

That these trees and their freight of knowledge were intended to interact in a dynamic way is clear. We have one figure, for example, of Jew, Christian and Muslim, each under the tree of his knowledge, and the thought of Lull as missionary, for he was also that, was that the Lullian art would lead to the peaceful harmonization of world religions in Christ. Unfortunately, how to work the art is not very clear, and later he will move to a system of dials which is closer to a modern computer, but explanations of its working by contemporary Lullians leave one with the awful feeling that they do not understand it themselves. That it, in a sense, did work is shown by his martyrdom in Tunis after a demonstration of its process and theological conculsions.

In any case, that the first effort at something like a computer should use the tree as model is natural on more than one ground. First, of course, because the branches and subdivisions provide a model of categorization vertically and horizontally, but second because it is (however otherwise awkward compared to a modern computer) a living thing, and the universe is, or at least was for people of older times, clearly a kind of organic unity.

The tree grows stage by stage, ring by ring. A great tree may seem to a reflective man, himself unprotected by bark and unsustained by roots, very close to immortality indeed, and sending its roots downward and branches upward, it participates in earth, sky and the underworld; and so naturally the Norse world-tree Yggdrassil, sends its roots down to Hel while its branches reach to high Asgard above, where the gods dwell.

A more subtle conception is that of the tree whose roots are above in the Divine world and among whose branches and leaves we live. We say "more subtle," yet it might occur to a child or to a man like St. Francis who, Chesterton remarks, seemed to see like a child standing on his head, how all things depend on God above. The Upanishads speak of such a tree, and the Jewish masters taught of the Tree of Life whose roots are above, with each soul below deriving from one of the high roots.

This Tree of Life was also a polarized descent of opposite qualities, the expansive movements of wisdom and kindness and the contractive of analysis and rigor, for example, with each in the process of interchange with its opposite... So for those teachers, the Tree is not just a static symbol, but something living and dynamic.

Now this model of the tree is the organic form of the hierarchical picture of the universe which C.S. Lewis writes of in *The Discarded Image*, and the idea of hierarchy is not an easy one for many people today to use and understand, though it is important for religious faith, not only of course for the question of what we have made of hierarchy in our churches, but more basically in understanding our place in the world and our way of access to God.

The problem is that in our day, hierarchy is pretty well limited to the sense of chain-of-command. So Simone Weil, in her subtle analysis of the needs of the soul as paired opposites (in The Need For Roots) opposes hierarchy and equality as two equal but opposite needs of the spirit. Valid though that is, it is an essentially modern understanding.

The ancient vision, or perhaps one should say, the *alternative* vision, for it still may be felt and held, starts with a dimension of 'height.' We, as C.S. Lewis observed, are with our radio telescopes aware of a vastly larger universe than the ancients knew. But if the Earth is small, so is everything else, and so what? But the other vision, of Dante for example, looks up into the night and sees sphere on sphere all the way back to the primum mobile, the high first stirrings of the universe, each greater and higher and more noble, so that the mind becomes dizzy with the abyss of height. If Pascal, allowing himself to see within the blinkers of modern sensibility, felt the terror of "the silence eternal and the space of infinity," for Dante, or anyone who sees into height, there is more the sense of being in an immense cathedral in whose ongoing building and beautification one had a specific place.

So when Dionysius, that mysterious sixth-century Syrian monk whose books exercised an enormous influence both in the east and in the west, writes his little books, *Celestial Hierarchy* and *Ecclesiastical Hierarchy*, he is speaking of a living, growing world, in which each of us stands in relation to the Most High and can participate in the Divine Life which flows like sap in a tree or like a river of light from the Eden above, down through all created things. Each degree of the order of the Universe, or of the Church, exists only to receive the flow of the Glory of God and pass it on in its integrity...so that, because each who receives also fully relinquishes (it is, Dionysius would say, the Law of the Kingdom) the light and glory is full and integral at every stage. There is a Hassidic saying which expresses this beautifully:

> The Most High is completely accessible from every rung of the ladder of Being.

The image is of an exchange and interchange, and is figured in the ladder Jacob saw, dreaming and aware, looking up into the night sky and seeing a ladder stretching up and up and on which the Angelicals, the bearers of the Glory, continually ascend and descend. An Angelic flow and return like that in the body of the arterial and venous blood,

Indeed Jesus, speaking to Bartholomew, says that it is he, the 'Son of Man' who is the Ladder of Earth and Heaven on which the angels ascend and descend. He is Himself the Tree of Life and the life of the tree, as he will say explicitly in the metaphor of the vine and branches:

> I am the vine and you are the branches.
>
> JOHN 15:1-5

And He goes on to say that those who share their lives with His, Divine-human life, will bear fruit on the Tree of Life.

The flow of the river of light and the interchange of life Divine and human (gods and men live each others' lives, as wise Heraclitus said): these are the laws of that order and hierarchy which Jacob and Dante saw, looking up into the night sky. These laws, the

laws of exchange, are remote from the average understanding of hierarchy today—perhaps very remote from the understanding of hierarchy by civil
bureaucrat or ecclesiastical hierarch—and yet they
remain surely the true laws of life, whose misunderstanding distorts both civic life and the life of the
Church. It is these laws, of hierarchy and exchange,
which we see imaged in all trees, and first in that great
Tree of Life whose roots are above, and in whose life
we too participate.

3

SWORD

THE LITTLE BOOK, *PILGRIM AT TINKER CREEK* by the American Christian poet Annie Dillard, is an altogether remarkable work. On one level it is observation over a year's course of nature in a mountain valley to the west of Virginia. But it is no more just that than Thoreau's *Walden* is only an account of a Massachusetts pond. It is perhaps first of all a deep meditation of the mystery of God's relation to the world. There is in Dillard a sense of the cruelty (at least according to our understanding) of nature 'red in tooth and claw,' of the falleness of nature, if you will, and she pursues this through an unblinking and rather appalling account of the terrible world of insects whose species make up, of course, a vast number of all living things.

If we wished to launch a modern meditation on the Fall from the point of view of its consequences in Nature, we could certainly start here...perhaps remembering (as Dillard does,) however, that what we see is but forms, and that an atom in some insect predator's brain might, split finally open, reveal a forest.

But just now I find myself thinking of an experience she recounts of watching the light on a mountainside. Light from beyond, and backlighting, the forest...Luminous as yet the shadows lengthen. She forgets herself for a timeless and a precious moment— which is many moments on the clock. What I am thinking about is this phenomenon, that our deepest moments of awareness of God or of the world can be moments where we are least aware of ourselves...

Music heard so deeply that it is not heard at all, but you are the music while the music lasts, as the poet says.

Adam in the garden sought the way to know himself and God at the same time. He seeks it still, and has not quite found it has he...? Have we?

The dervishes sit on cushions in a circle, chanting the affirmation of the Unity:

La illahillah la...

Originally, this was an affirmation on behalf of a local god known as Allah, but in the Sufi vision it deepens and becomes,

There is no Reality but God.

No true Reality outside of Him. Affirmation, and beyond it nothing. So it is said that a Sheikh chanting "There is no..." disappeared and became visible again as his chant finished, "but God," and so he winked on and off like some cosmic blinker as the song went on.

This time of singing is called 'The Sword of Light,' and it is said that a sword is whirling in the air which will cut off the head of anyone who stands before the chant ends...

The paradox seems to be that God made us thinking beings, creatures of mind to think and words to describe, and He made Himself known to us supremely and finally as the Word... And yet it is only when our ordinary flow of thought is interrupted that we are able to stand at the edge of the world of spiritual knowledge...But how can we know if the Sword of Light has severed our thought from itself? –As one translation renders it,

> I have posted a sword at every gate, to flash like lightning.
>
> EZEKIEL 21:15

Annie Dillard has no answers, just the experience of light illuminating a tree, at a moment when she forgot to remember herself...a moment which passes too quickly. I know this moment, and it is difficult to speak of experiences because in ways each person's are different, so that, one can quickly, with talk of spiritual experience, feel left out, or leave the other out without intention. But this moment of feeling that which is outside of myself, and at the same moment beginning to lose that precious, direct, unmediated knowledge by stepping in its way, stepping between myself and God...this moment I do know. And likely in one way or another you do too.

I think (once Fr. Alexander Schmemann said to me, perhaps trying to play the part of the whirling sword, "You think too much," when I started a sentence thus, but it is my nature to start things so, as another may start with, "I feel"), I think we each need to work with this problem, with these paradoxes, that God is known by thought...and what thought begins when all thought ends?

Not a lot is written about this. That is to say, not a lot picks up where Annie Dillard leaves off...

When the sun has set behind the mountain...

4

KINGDOM

THE CATHOLIC THEOLOGIAN JOHN S. DUNNE points out that at some time in one's life everyone comes to the point where the question arises: What kind of story is this story I am living in?

The question occurred to Gilgamesh at the very dawn of history when his friend died, and he began a journey to find a place beyond death and beyond the decay which, as the third law of thermodynamics tells us and his sorrow told him, makes all things fall and all systems fail. In the end, having even crossed the waters of death, Gilgamesh returns with the dark knowledge that immortality is only in the gift of the gods. No learned wisdom is made explicit in this strange story: at most it might have been that of the dark words inscribed on the poet Yeats' tomb:

Cast a cold eye on life, on death,
Horseman pass by!

Yet the search for the Garden continues.

I have travelled from the west to the east, and from the east to the west again, in search of the lost word...

Haunting words—maybe too deep for the banal Masonic ritual in which they are embedded.

In the twelfth century when Constantinople was, as ever, hard pressed by the forces of the Prophet, a Bishop Hugh of Jabala in Syria brought word of a Christian priest-king in the east who had successfully waged war against the Muslims, in effect, to the rear of their Asian extension. That welcome news, to a land which had little but defense and retreat to show for the war of centuries, was followed in 1165 by a letter addressed to the Emperor Manuel Comnenus written, as it seemed, by John himself.

> If indeed you wish to know wherein consists our great power, then believe without doubting that I, Prester John ,who reign supreme, exceed in riches, virtue and power all creatures who dwell under heaven. Seventy-two kings pay tribute to me. I am a devout Christian...and have made a vow to visit the Sepulchre of the Lord with a great army as befits the glory of our majesty, and to make war against the enemies of the Cross... Our magnificence dominates the three Indias, to the farther India where the body of St. Thomas rests, through the desert to the rising sun...

He goes on to describe his land, including two rivers full of jewels and a marvelous plate hanging in his palace, which 'by the Grace of the Holy Spirit' provides whatever food one wants.

Now of course the letter was a hoax (perhaps written in Italy) and the whole seems a novelistic echo in the west of certain events in the east, the Nestorian missions and the Mongol lords who for a time were Christian, and a Mongol victory in 1141 in which the Kara-Kitai crushed the Seljuk Turks at a great battle near fabled Samarkand. But the thing was believed in its time and for long exercised an imperious influence both on the spiritual and romantic imagination, for example, of Wolfram Von Eschenbach, who at the end of *Parzival* has the Grail depart to the land of the Priest-King in the east, and on the practical and political imagination as well. The quest for a linkup with a Christian power in the east for long played a part in Portuguese colonial expansion into the Indies and then, for a branch of the Prester John story leads there, into Africa. The African dimension is reflected in John Buchan's classic thriller *Prester John*.

It is finally Eden which is being sought, and the Edenic nature of Prester John's kingdom is shown in that the river Physon, one of the rivers of the Garden, according to Genesis, flows in its midst. The land of the Priest-King is in the same general (and vaguely central Asian) area as the Tibetan legendary land of Shambhalla, which becomes Shangrila in James Hilton's novel. Shambhalla for Tibetans is an object of search by geographic wandering through the mountains, a quest joined by the strange modern Russian mystic Nicholas Roerich who managed to obtain funding from the US Department of Agriculture in the 1930s on the pretext that he was doing an agricultural survey, and to this may be joined the effort by dream and meditation to somehow reach that city from its astral and inner side. It is said that the supreme mandala diagrams of wisdom are openly displayed in that city and just to see them is to receive enlightenment.

The theme not only of Eden but of Kingdom is taken up along eccentric lines by St. Yves de Alveydre who, in *Mission d'l'Indie* supposes a system of tunnels under the oceans leading to the land of the 'King of the World.' The idea of such a hidden universal King is taken seriously by the modern philosopher Rene Guenon, who was a brilliant and serious if eccentric thinker and guru of the 'Traditionalists,' and the Polish explorer Ferdinand Ossendowski sought his land, that of the city Aggartha, as he wandered in Mongolia in 1920. He found instead a figure as strange as any 'King of the World:' the barbarous White Russian general Ungern von Sternberg, who regarded himself as the reincarnation of Genghis Khan and, as far as possible, played the part. Later lying in the Gobi desert, Ossendowski does hear some sound, seemingly subterranean, which may, he suggests, have been from the hidden land.

There have been other geographic quests, from the Celtic voyages, including the famous voyage of St. Brendan, in search of the Isles of the Blessed, to a curious little allegorical novel, *Mount Analog,* written by the French Gurdjievan Rene Daumal in our time. "Seek refuge within, poor wanderer," admonishes one of Roualt's Miserère series—a picture of a wanderer bent from travel and from not finding what he sought.

So of course we may find that the quest of the Hesychast for the Place of the Heart, which he seeks not with the measured tread of his feet, but by his measured breath, is that same journey of Gilgamesh in search of Eden. For it is not the physical organ which is the Heart they seek, but an inner point or moment of balance where mind and heart resolve in integral being. So Macarius says that at this absolute center, there are unfathomable depths:

> God is there in the angels, light and life, the Kingdom and the Apostles, the heavenly cities and the treasures of Grace...

All things are there. So the mystics who sought, by meditation, to ride the Chariot of Elijah to Paradise, were called 'Those Who Descend in the Chariot,' for the way they found was within. Marsilio Ficino, priest and master of the Platonic Academy in the Florence of the Medici, saw the stars and constellations mirrored within.

Yet for many the travel within, as well as the travel without can be weariness. The inner cities and stars prove no more accessible than the Land of Prester John, and one takes the road home again with no more than the bitter wisdom of the old Sumerian Gilgamesh. Yet does not the word that he brought back, that immortality is in the gift of the Divine, open up another perspective? Perhaps the perspective of receiving as gift what one cannot obtain by seeking?

A Japanese Pilgrim's song:

A far far distant land
Is paradise,
I've heard them say
But those who want to go
May get there in a day!

And the novelist and Presbyterian minister, Fredrich Buechner, who wrote a novel of St. Brendan's strange journey by sea to seek paradise, lay on the grass straining somehow inwardly towards God, to hear God's voice, and all at once out of the still sky he heard two branches strike: *clack-clack!* In that moment this opened his mind to the realization that God is speaking to us, is present to us, through every sound and sight, through the whole range of the created world. Through all of this, all of this *clack-clack*, we are present, if we will be, in the Eden above even now and here and always.

There is a drawing by the curious old artist Michael Mayer, Lutheran and alchemist, showing a scholar seeking truth with a lantern. While Truth walks ahead in daylight amid beauty and wonder, the scholar is bent over seeking to trace her footprints in the midst of a darkness, so little illuminated by his poor lamp, which surrounds and accompanies only him. It is an image for pilgrims, and who of us is not a pilgrim and stranger, as the Scripture says, to ponder perhaps...

5

SHEMA

THIS LITTLE MEDITATION BEGINS on a September Monday night. We are gathered for Bible study in Manyasha's apartment on the north side of Moscow, and as people come in, Andrey strums the guitar...

Shema O Israyel,
Adonai Elihenu! Adonai Ehad!
Hear O Israel,
The Lord your God, the Lord is One!

Now someone may say that this song, which even today is at the heart of Jewish morning and evening worship, is not properly ours. It is something we are doing to show, perhaps, our inclusiveness...but it does not belong to us Christians. Is it not even, the confession of the Unity, a kind of denial of the Trinity? A rejection of the Christian vision? At the least it is of the Old Testament, now superseded by the worship of the Trinity.

Someone might say this, but why do my eyes fill with tears as the song builds to the final *ehad?* —Which in Bloch's orchestral arrangement becomes an explosion: *Adonai...EHAD!*

23

The 'gift of tears' is, by the way, not really something to pray for. It is a curious gift, if gift it is, always rather embarrassing, and one feels a bit of a fool. (A friend who warned me of this, back in dry-eyed days, added that for this reason on Good Friday he must always seek a place in the back of the church behind a pillar). At the word *Ehad* itself, and just for a moment, a blink of an eye, an immeasurable depth seems to open, a depth without end... How can I endure this word which is too great for me? And I feel a kind of vertigo.

But why, if this is something superseded, do I feel this emotion? It must be in part the awareness of a lost oneness...in ourselves, in myself, in the world.

The story is told, (we will use a Jewish narration which comes from a deep meditation of Genesis), Adam was clothed in light, yet somehow, whereas children grow out of their clothes, he diminished, and his clothes were shattered and the shards of light became the worlds. And Adam himself was somehow shattered. It is said that the *Shekinah*, the Presence of God, wanders the world in search of the shreds of light, to gather them. And Adam also, in his exile, seeks to find himself, the way back to himself. It is the story of Abraham, of Isaac and Jacob, isn't it? And then St. Paul tells us of the one who was Adam before Adam, and who alone can show Adam his restored

face... It is the Master who in his last prayer asks
that they may all be *EHAD*. I in them and they in me.
So the prayer, the high-priestly prayer as it is called,
goes deeper than the unity of the Church and of the
dispersed families of Christ...though I think it sees
ahead to that time when we are one, and includes and
demands it, (may it come speedily and in our time! —
You may say 'Amen'). But it is a deeper thing, which
also gives that demanded unity of the churches a
deeper dimension.

It is the restored unity of Adam, the recovery of
wholeness, which we recover in ourselves and through
each other, and first in Christ: "I in them and they in
me."

God is always and at every moment and point only
One. This is our faith...expressed in the *Shema,* or the
Shahada (called by the Sufis 'The Sword of Light') of
Islam.

Then out of our brokenness, Adam's brokenness,
comes the ground for the revelation of Trinity, which
seals the possibility of persons who are themselves
and who yet are within the Unity. For when we look
into the Unity, where will we find a place to be?
Who shall stand when he appeareth?
MALACHI 3:1
Adam could not know himself and the Unity at the
same time...and he was shattered,

25

For nothing can be sole or whole
that has not first been rent...

W.B. YEATS

The Master shows us the way, He is The Way, of the coinherence, of the Trinity, which is also the way of unity...that they be One. The Coinherence of persons is Community...the mirror of the Trinity. When the Church is Community (not only in the future, but now, already) it is *EHAD*. That is the Unity for which the Lord prays...before and after and in the depth of the formal unity which it is also our task to show the world. But it is finally only this unity of persons, revealing the Trinity, and based on the *EHAD*, the Divine Unity...only this can answer the prayer that 'they may be one...that the world may believe.' A formal unity of Churches, good and important that may be, will not compel belief—only a unity of persons.

These thoughts, then on the Shema: how it is our prayer and inseparable from the Lord's final prayer. And now the chords of the guitar change, a little lighter, but full of majesty and glory,

Laudate Dominum! Omnes Gentes, Alleluia!

6

HERMIT

ADVICE IS A DANGEROUS THING to give and some of the reasons are summed up nicely by one of Tolkien's immortal elves:

> Elves seldom give unguarded advice, for advice is
> a dangerous gift, even from the wise to the wise, and
> all courses may run ill...

However, it is hard to resist the demand, or temptation, to give advice and the elf goes on:

> Yet if you demand advice I will give it
> for friendship's sake.

And indeed a great deal of advice, most of it on the whole good, is given throughout *The Lord of the Rings*, by elves, by wizards, by dwarves, by men and even by living trees.

Similarly, in the Grail stories, the questing knights seem to find each day a hermitage in the forest where an amiable and wise hermit will interpret their dreams, hear their confession of sin and give them absolution, and even (in the case of young Parsival) give instructions in social ettiquette and table manners.

Nor is this only a habit of the Catholic-minded. The resolutely Protestant John Bunyan tells us that his

Pilgrim stops first, after his conversion, at the house of Interpreter who explains his experience of New Birth to him and tells him something of the road ahead, where indeed he will no more than a Grail Knight lack for advisors on the way.

Now it must be that we write so in our literature because we experience this in our own journey through life, or perhaps because we wish that we did. I recall myself as a child hearing *Pilgrim's Progress*, for my mother read it to me, and I am glad that she did, though I am also glad that she read *Alice in Wonderland* too, to balance the picture of the road of life ahead, and I remember wishing that life were as clearly marked out as Pilgrim's way seemed to be; even then I had doubts of it.

So also do many who undertake a spiritual discipline, wish for advice and for guidance—for a Spiritual Director, or for an Elder (*Starets* or *Geron* in the terminology of the East), who will perhaps prescribe a rule of life and monitor and attest to one's progress. This can be a little, of course, like the elderly person whose social life consists of visits to the doctor. But it often is of the deepest seriousness. In any case, almost every religion and spiritual grouping has at least one stream which emphasizes an absolute need for spiritual guidance in order to make progress.

In the Eastern tradition, Nicetas says:

> Not to submit oneself to a spiritual father, in imitation
> of the Son who was obedient to his Father, is not to
> be born from above.

It is often said also, and beyond the general direction
of life, that specific disciplines, for example the Prayer
of Jesus, should not be undertaken without direction.

Yet it seems that how to receive direction is not
always self-evident. One comes to a clearing in the
forest, but there is no hermit's hut in sight. The
nineteenth-century Russian philosopher, Kireevsky
says that there is one thing more precious than all else
in life, and that is to find a genuine Russian Elder who
will open and clarify one's heart and motives and
path. But implicit in this is that such a director is not
easily and everywhere to be found. So the poet
Alexander Blok regarded as his spiritual guide and
elder, the writer Vladimir Soloviev with whom he
never spoke and only saw once. That sight was so
striking, of the aging Soloviev in his fur coat with wild
hair and beard and looking like a silhouette, Blok will
remember, of a figure from another dimension, that in
the experience Block found his elder.

Sometimes it would seem that this difficulty of
finding guidance in the inner way is deliberately
pointed up by those, in the Church, who have no great
interest in mystical and inner journeys. For example

in the form: "To do that (e.g. practice the Prayer of Jesus) you need good spiritual direction from a monk who knows something about it." And then: "But unfortunately in our time and place there aren't any such monks." There may be a good deal of practical sense, even of spiritual practical sense, in discouraging mystical enthusiasms, and yet one remembers the Master's word against those who block the access of others to doors they have not entered themselves. "You can't get there from here," are words one might hesitate to say lightly.

What resolution can we propose? Perhaps we may say first that for most people what is needed is not so much knowledge of a way as an example of it. So in relation to the Jesus Prayer it is sometimes said that one needs specialized direction in the technique. Or those who practice Fr. John Main's method of 'Christian Meditation' are invited to listen to various series of tapes outlining that method. Yet in both these cases, and in others as well, the actual matter passed on is very simple and available enough in books. However, what is needed is a living example. It is hard to be a Christian if one has never seen the Christian life lived by another. It is hard to believe in the importance of prayer if one has never known a man of prayer. And while one may accept, and know in one's heart the truth of the poignant force of Leon

Bloy's profound word, "The only sadness is to not be a saint," how can one approach sanctity without some living model or exemplar?

This role of the Hermit in the forest, or the elder, as exemplar is separate from, and I would say both more important and harder to replace than, that of teacher or initiator. One may receive initiation and teaching from the books, yet no book can show the living way to holiness. When the elder exemplifies the spiritual way, it opens out as a living possibility for the first time, and as they say, a picture is worth a thousand words.

So the force of the Russian classic *Way of a Pilgrim* comes not least from the sense of meeting, in the pilgrim, a living person, and that renders this little book far more accessible than are the treatises designed to teach the same way of prayer.

Now it seems to me that in every aspect of our involvement with the Divine we are at risk of missing what is actually there, and what God is sending us, in looking for something else. If I look again at the person next to me in line at the supermarket, perhaps he is the Hermit, at least at this moment and at least for me. This realization is at the core of the spiritual way of the contemporary French writer who called himself 'Sedir' (an anagram for *desir*, 'spiritual desire'). Sedir says, that after all possible spiritual explorations,

> ...Alchemists admitted me to their laboratories and Sufis, Buddhists and Taoists many nights have taken me to the abode of their gods...

After all this he meets a man, a simple Christian known as 'Master Phillip' who had only two books: the *Bible* and *The Imitation of Christ,* and,

> All that these admirable men had taught me became as ethereal as the mist which rises at dusk from the overheated earth.

And he says:

> Let us love our brothers as ourselves and we shall find him [the 'Unknown' as Sedir refers to this exemplar who is there for us]. He may be working alongside of us, he may be that man at the subway entrance who lets himself be pushed aside by an impatient commuter. He may be the passerby leaning over the parapets of the Seine, or the man there walking along the dams.

With attention we may find, in other words, the 'Unknown,' the Hermit, the Elder, and find him perhaps in many places, in many brothers and sisters or, if our way requires it, in unique intensity from one or another sister or brother. It seems it is attention which is needed to validate the formula,

> When the disciple is ready the master appears.

Of course it is the pattern of all perception of the Divine: here , now, God is Speaking... Creating... Loving... But then there must be one more side to it, to the Mystery of spiritual guidance, and of finding him, and that is that we are also he, if we will, and perhaps even without our willing of it. Are we not in a place to be somehow example and exemplar for someone, and to allow ourselves to be the 'Unknown?' We open ourselves to see and to receive, but then we also open ourselves to give... So the dictum reverses and also holds,

When the Master is ready the disciple appears.

And then, with this opening of our eyes, we see that the old stories are true... There are, after all, hermits in the forest, and there, that must be the house of Interpreter. And more important yet, that there, in the face of that brother I saw the flickering fire of holiness in that moment, and remembered myself and my way and what is at the end of the way beyond all hope.

7

SILENCE

OFTEN IN CHRISTIAN HISTORY the question of the language of the Liturgy has been posed. It has been raised in terms of whether there should be a universal language, Latin, or whether the vernacular should be used. Or should a period in the development of a language be, in effect, canonized as the sacred language? This can be the question of Church Slavonic in Russia, or the preference for 'Holy Ghost' over 'Holy Spirit' in the hills of Tennessee. But the assumption is that Liturgy is made up simply of language, and yet we may press beyond this a little when we start with the realization that every spoken and proclaimed and prayed and intoned word rises out of silence. Silence is formally the ground of Liturgy, as it is of all speech and prayer, but what is the significance of this for the understanding of that prayer?

Fr. John Breck says,

> proclamation and celebration of the Word must resolve into Silence...for Silence to become the matrix of revelation, it must assume its own objective reality...not merely the absence of sound.

And the *Wisdom of Solomon* tells us,

> when deep silence enveloped all things...the Royal Word...leapt down from heaven. [8:14]

Yet while our Christian tradition knows many considerations of silence and individual prayer (within the Eastern tradition it is at the heart of hesychasm) it seems almost nothing has been written on the significance of Silence as matrix of Word within liturgical prayer and in particular the Liturgy of the Eucharist, which is the most central expression of our prayer.

So perhaps we may suggest some possible directions for thought, and also suggest the possible significance of pursuing this thought.

To speak about Silence is to deal with something which cannot easily be discussed…"One cannot discuss it as other subjects," as Plato says in the seventh letter of the ineffable. Yet perhaps, as the philosopher goes on to say, as one works with it as one can, "a flame leaps across…like a fire kindled by a spark." We intend not so much a scholarly discourse then, but to light a spark and share its blaze.

As background we use, and suggest, the book *The World of Silence*, by the Swiss Christian philosopher Max Picard. This amazing meditation was published in 1946 and it is still almost the only serious work on Silence as such, although there are suggestive materials in Rudolph Otto's *Das Helige*, and also in Thomas Merton. In Kierkegaard and Heidegger, Silence is sought… It breathes in the poetry of Rilke…of Eliot.

Now, if Silence is the matrix of the Word, then it is also there even when there is speech. It has an autonomous reality as ground of the Liturgy and is only made more perceptible by the cessation of sound. Furthermore, each person brings his interior and personal silence into the Liturgy... But our silence outside of prayer is very different from the silence of God. It is a silence based on our awareness of what we have lost and of what we have desired but never had, and of our death, and it is deeply penetrated by darkness But the real Silence, that of God, is full of Spirit and Light...

The Eucharist, completing the Mystery of Baptism, is an offering of our life, in return for the Divine Life. As we speak the words of prayer, we are also giving up our life, returning the word to God (from whom we received it) and passing into the silence which is also our acceptance of our death, of giving up our lives to God, confident that He will return Life. "This is the meaning of death," says Abraham Heschel, "the ultimate self-dedication to the divine... This act of giving away is reciprocity on man's part for God's gift of life. For the pious man it is a privilege to die." And then God returns Life to us by replacing our word with His Word. And so the heart of the Liturgy is exchange of word and silence, of our word out of our silence for God's Word, out of the Silence which is full of Resurrection...the exchange of death and Life.

From this primordial structure of the Liturgy it follows that the contradictions of individuals which rise when we speak out of our individual silences (shot through with darkness), are resolved. They are resolved in that Word which is spoken out of true Silence, and so Community is created in Liturgy, which makes possible the speaking of word out of silence.

As we realize this depth of Silence out of which Liturgy is prayed, we realize then (not just as theory) the 'Power of His Resurrection' [PHIL.3:10], which is its heart. In the words of St. Isaac of Syria:

Silence is the Sacrament of the world to come.

•

There is a remarkable Buddhist text which I believe (within the light of Silence) is completed by the Liturgy, and which in turn illuminates the deep structure of Christian Liturgy. It is from the *Prajnaparamita Sutra* (Heart of Wisdom):

Emptiness is Form!
and Form is precisely Emptiness!
This is the great Incantation!
The incantation which dispels all Fear!
...Oh what a realization! [or Awakening]
All Hail! [Bodhi Svaha!]

But the conception of 'Emptiness' is of pregnant Silence...a matrix of Life and reality and so we may transpose...(And I have consulted on the validity of this with people who are learned in Buddhism.)

Silence is Word

and Word is precisely Silence!

And the joy of realization, whose quality of delight is evident in the Buddhist text but its source left in Mystery, is seen to be fulfilled in Resurrection and in Liturgy. For the exchange and interpenetration between emptiness and form is grounded as it is also fulfilled, in the death and Resurrection of Christ, and finds its focal point in the Chalice. But again if the Liturgy fulfills all that was sought through the 'Gates of Silence' (Fr. Alexander Men's title of his study of Buddhism), yet in turn the joy rising from the interchange of emptiness and form can perhaps illumine our understanding of what comes from Silence and Word...the exchanged death and Life... Oh what a realization! All Hail!

I believe it is worth underlining what is possible here... it is not simply a possible more-or-less exact analogy betwee the Buddhist thought and thestructure of the Eucharist in its depth, but also the illumination of the Liturgy which the awareness of its philosophical depths bring. For at least some minds it may be a way of joining understanding to faith, in a flash of realization. 'A flame leaps across...'

Liturgy then, is Silence and Word. The Hassids said that God wrote the Law in Black Fire on a ground of White Fire and that at the end it will be seen that the true Law is in the

White Fire as well as in the Black. In Liturgy, God speaks His Word of Black Fire on the ground of His Silence...which is White Fire.

So finally, let us suggest some consequences of these things. Perhaps they can be the technical consequence, if one may so express it, of seeking to restore more spaces in our prayer where Silence, which underlies the whole Liturgy, is apparent. In the Eastern Liturgy we may say that there are moments of this sort at the Great Entrance (especially in the Liturgy of the Presanctified Gifts), but not many such moments. The liturgy of Taizé in the west is an example of a modern Liturgy which seeks to set word in a space... to make Silence manifest. In the west also, the whole cult of the Adoration takes place within the context of Silence and I would suggest (against some modern western scholars who regard it as anti-clerical, which of course has been the normative eastern thought also), that it is this which suggests that it comes from the heart of Liturgy.

There can be, anyway, in the celebration of Liturgy a discovery and remembering of Silence which is reflected in the celebration, in the priest's serving and in the choir and through the whole...and this without any specific reordering or reforming of the Liturgy.

Isaiah cries,

> Woe to those who join house to house and field to
> field until there is no space remaining.

This may be applied also to the running of word into word without space. For although the Silence remains (as we said) behind and under the words, the problem is that in this way of praying an attitude is reflected... the attitude that the words themselves are the whole of the prayer. From this profound misunderstanding there arises then an absolutizing of the forms of the words... perhaps of the liturgical language but in any case of the externality of the word of prayer. The Prophet Isaiah goes on to say that those who buy all of the properties so that there is no space between will be left in a terrible solitude. We may, allegorically, but surely truly, say that those who absolutize the form will be left with empty churches and the solitude of their false absolutism. At the same time, the restoration of the awareness of Silence as underlying Word, opens the way to freedom from this inauthentic absolutism, just as in dogmatic theology the apophatic principle—itself a theology of silence—frees us from false contradictions in our understanding of doctrine.

Then, more deeply, as we discover that Silence is not first of all that of personal prayer (and Hesychia) but...while it is that, is that as deriving from... the Silence which together with the Word is the heart of Liturgy, we will find that the end of all personal spiritual quests, and the resolution of all our impossible contradictions ('the great incantation which dispels all fear!') is here at the beginning of everything...at the Lord's table, gathered together. Here it is at the place where all Christian prayer begins...'In the beginning is my end,' says the poet T.S. Eliot, expressing this, and,

> The end of all our exploring
> Will be to arrive where we started
> And know the place for the first time.
> Through the unknown, remembered, gate...

The Gate of Silence.

And this becomes, as we have said, the ground of that self-discovery and self-disclosure of the Church which is Community. Community made possible by the deep structure of Prayer, of Silence before the Word, and of Word from Silence...

May the Holy Spirit grant that as we consider these things which indeed 'are not like other things,'

> A flame leaps across!

And (Eliot again)

> (Light) has answered...to Light
> and is Silent...
> the light is Still.

8

HERON

Emptiness and Form, Silence and Word.
Gabriel Marcel hesitates to accept
silence as more than absence, emptiness
as more than negation... How shall I not
hestitate?

"Look at the bird!" a woman cries.

There in a shallow pond is a small heron...
a snowy egret... moving its long legs deliberately
through the water and then poising, white and
crested,
itself beyond doubting in that moment, both
Form and Emptiness.

It is Silence.

It itself is Word.

9

Dove

Once, a Russian folk tale relates, a great book fell to earth from a thundercloud. It was hundreds of feet in length and width and the people were unable to open and read it until it disclosed something of its meaning to a wise king, who explained to the gathered people that the universe is the garment of God. But no man, not even the wisest, could read the book. The title of that book, which must represent the mystery of Nature, was *The Book of the Dove.*

There is a 'Book of the Dove' by the Syrian Bar Hebraeus (1226-1286), which indeed can be opened and read. It is a very small book and hard to find, but it too has its mysteries.

Bar Hebraeus was the last and perhaps the most brilliant of the great Syriac writers. His work is in a wide range of genres, from a history of the world, to humor, to an encyclopedia. In chapter four of his *Book of the Dove* he tells something of his inner life.

When he was young he studied and argued theology with other Christians, but then he came to see the differences as not worth the hatred he saw them engender,

> I became convinced that these quarrels of Christians among themselves are not a matter of facts, but of words and semantics...and I wholly eradicated the root of hatred from the depth of my heart and absolutely forsook disputation with anyone regarding confession.

Then he turned to logic and mathematics, astronomy and physics and metaphysics:

> Because life is short and learning long and broad, I read concerning every branch of science only what was most necessary.

He learned that

> the colors of the rainbow are only caused by density and rarefaction, compactness and transparency.

I recall one of my early science teachers teaching this to us, and drawing the simple materialist lesson from it that therefore we ought not feel a sense of wonder when we look at the rainbow, since all it is is light refracted. But Bar Hebraeus derives from this rather that the wonder of the source of light is something greater, and other, than the colors of the refracted image.

Yet what science could not do, incline him to doubt, the words of the theologians did. He fell towards unbelief, for the words of the theologians of his time seemed all nulls, or 'simple thoughts without effect.' Then,

> Some of the rays of light without limit came on me like the flash of lightning and my eyes opened a little and I saw more but only partly... Now without

44

> ceasing I pray that all that impedes my sight
> yet may be destroyed and eye to eye I may
> behold the beloved... The following few sentences
> are a part of what I saw in the flash of lightning...

And there follow one hundred paragraphs of the genre of the 'Century' so common in that time. Some of them are conventional, here and there is something remarkable:

> I found myself in the light of light, my limbs relaxed,
> my mind vanished and I was like a man on a
> runaway stallion, or flying through the air...

And sometimes there is something wise and earned from his experience as well as from illumination: this, concerning 'teachers and sages, exoteric and esoteric,'

> When I see that they have dared to weigh all in
> their scale their boast does not seem beautiful
> to me, for though their scale seems just and
> right, it does not contain the multitude of things
> of the world to come.

But at the end he says,

> Speech already wearies me, while my heart
> tends to what is more expedient.

And finally one more word...(There is the book from the thunder cloud, and here in this little book of the Syrian is the lightning of illumination, but after the thunder and the lightning flash, surely this too is the voice of the Dove...)

> I realized that a man can receive nothing except
> as gift.

10

FOLLY

HOLY FOLLY (*YURODSTVO*) IS AN OBVIOUS and important strand in the weave of Russian Christianity. Indeed St. Basil's Cathedral on Red Square in Moscow, whose fantastic towers and cupolas and variegated colors make it look like a some image of Shangrila or perhaps a decoration on a wonderful wedding cake, is dedicated not, as one would expect, to St. Basil of Cappadocia, the compiler of an Orthodox liturgy, but to a Russian 'Fool in Christ.'

Typically Russian as *yurodstvo* was to be, perhaps the first of the Russian fools was a German merchant who came to Novgorod and we are told was converted to Orthodoxy, like many another after him, first of all by the sense of the beauty of the Holy he found in 'the rich ornaments, the holy singing, the great chime of the bells.' After being baptized with the name Procopius (late in the thirteenth century) he decided:

> I do not wish corruptible glory, and so shall go wandering in eastern countries.

He passed, as George Fedotov tells the story in *Russian Religious Mind*, through 'towns and villages, impervious

impervious forests and swamps.' It was a rough life, as the life of a vagabond always is, in many ways maybe not unlike that of the American Depression-era hoboes and vagabonds romanticized in song and in the fiction of the time. People beat Procopius, the frost and the snow were cruel, and finally, driven by a group of beggars from a hut where he has taken refuge, he is lying near death when an Angelical appears in the form of a youth who gives him some flowers, 'and immediately the scent of the flowers entered my heart and strengthened me.' Later he will become accepted in his wanderings and be known as a sort of prophet; for example people noticed that when the three pokers he habitually held in one hand were pointed up, there would be a good crop that season, while when they were held parallel to the ground the harvest would be bad. The life of St Procopius is typical perhaps of the lives of the Russian fools, in that it shows the bright coloration of folk painting, combined with some darker undertones.

There can be, certainly in the person who chooses, or who is impelled into, this way, some underlying wound of spirit, and as Nicholas Arseniev observes (in *Russian Piety*) holiness can also manifest together with psychic disorder. But perhaps first of all the Fool was a kind of 'outsider.' There are other kinds, and perhaps more common in our literature and experience is the bitter outsider, whom we find as the *picaro* ,the man who lives by his wits, celebrated in the Spanish picaresque novels. Willie Loman, in *Death of a Salesman*, would be a contemporary example of the outsider living by his wits, or more darkly, Harry Lime of *The Third Man* who goes so far outside as to sell watered penicillin with tragic results. Perhaps the same sort of person who may become a *picaro* might become a 'fool,' the psychological background may be quite similar. Surely the difference is in the choice of where to place one's trust. The clever man trusts in himself and his poor store of wit and device, the fool trusts in God.

Though the Russian fools were to form a class of society in a way unknown in any other country, holy folly is by no means limited to Russia. The type of 'Fool in Christ' is surely just as clearly manifest in St. Benedict Joseph Labre, the wanderer, as it is in Procopius or those who came after him. Furthermore, there is a folly and cosmic playfulness throughout the life of St. Francis of Assisi, the poor man and troubadour of God. For that matter, in the East we have the stories of Zen fools like the Chinese poet called 'Cold Mountain' *(Kanzan)* or the warm and winsome character of the poet Ryokan, drinking sake and playing ball with the children.

Moreover, is it not a wind of Divine Folly which blows through the incomparable music of *The Magic*

Flute? And the gaunt visage of Don Quixote who forever rides the dusty roads of La Mancha—is this not the face of the holy fool? The Fool becomes a playing card in Italy, sometimes named *Amor*.... an identification of mysteries reflected in the love of Harlequin for Columbine in the Comedia del Arte.

Now I suppose folly, like humor, has at least two components: exuberance and incongruity, and both of these resonate to the heart of religious experience, do they not? Exuberance is the experience of things as ever new, and ever renewed in God's ever-beginning Creation. The world is always amazing and fresh to the religious heart, the heart of the fool certainly, which knows that every day is the first day of Creation.

Beyond this there is incongruity, which can be the source of that bitter humor which points up the terrible and yet terribly funny, gap between what is and what ought be; it is 'laughter through tears,' or instead of tears. So Freud regarded humor to be essentially a transformation of hostility. But there is another and deeper kind of incongruity which arises from the many levels of Reality. For the world as we experience it in the daily newspaper is quite a different thing from the world in its ground in God, and when one is accustomed to seeing only one of these dimensions, the flat dimension of every day, and suddenly meets an intimation of the Divine in its full multi-dimensionality, one will be struck by the incongruity of a figure whose outline one will be as surely unable to grasp as would a two dimensional 'Flatlander' (thinking of Edward Abbot's admirable fantasy *Flatland*) be unable to comprehend the appearance in his world of a three dimensional hand. It is in this sense that Don Quixote is forever incongruous.

One may say that in some sense Holy Folly is present wherever religious truth breaks through into time, just as ionization accompanies the lightning flash. Surely also the Mystery of Folly, in this deep sense (not in the neurasthenic forms which often, in Russia for example, accompanied its manifestation), is peculiarly central to Christianity, whose heart, after all, is that ultimate incongruity, the Deity in Time... the impossible union of the worlds in Incarnation. Further, there is the Folly of Christ's self-emptying, or *kenosis*, which becomes the pattern to the humility of a St. Sergius, who is mistaken for a gardener, or of a St. Francis, whose 'perfect joy' is in his emptiness, that alone which he has to offer his God. And is it not the Fool, whose name is Amor, who acts through Maxmilian Kolbe offering himself for another at Treblinka, or Mother Maria Skobtsova likewise going in substitution to the gas chambers at Ravensburg?

What is more foolish, from the point of view of the world of superfices, than the thought that a biped in a decaying body when emptied of all else is found to be imperishable...'immortal diamond?'

Folly, present, as ionization accompanies the lightning, even today...

Wesley must have seemed a perfect fool to Oxford when he there announced himself 'Pastor to the World.' And C. S. Lewis after all would explain to the raised eyebrows of a later Oxford how he had not been a believer when he got into the sidecar of his brother Warnie's motorcycle, but by the time they reached the zoo he was a convert—a remarkable event considering the nature of a ride in a motorcycle sidecar! They were marginalized at Oxford, the Lewises and the Williamses and their ilk, but they learned humbly to use the margins and find there the freedom to speak to the world...

I asked a friend who knew Helene Iswolsky and others of that remarkable 'Third Hour' circle which met in New York after World War II—a group which included at various times Jaques Maritain, Pastor Schenk, W. H. Auden, Fr. Schmemann, Bishop John Shahavskoy, Dorothy Day, and Catherine deHueck— what he thought was the defining element which held together all these people, of such diverse personal character and ecclesiastical commitment? He replied, after a little thought, that they all had in common, if in various degrees and styles, a certain Holy Folly, an awareness of the utter incongruity of such a grouping of Mere Christians. It would be incongruous enough today, and this was before Vatican II. The group demonstrated an acceptance of that incongruity, of that folly, if you will.

Perhaps, beyond expectation then, the light which reflects from the bright domes of St. Basil's, and illumines the road of La Mancha, may also, fall on the roads of our life if we will accept the incongruity of it... of standing, and of appearing as one who so stands appears, in a light whose source is east of the sun...

11

FIRE

IRINA YAZIKOVA IS A BRILLIANT ICONOLOGIST and she also has a strong interest in Charismatic Renewal. Icon painting can be regarded as a somewhat static art in which the artist's choices are rather deliberately limited, unless it be in the folk forms such as Rumanian glass painting, and I asked her, with some curiosity, how she saw the relation of the Holy Spirit to iconography. As it happened she was to speak, on the following day, at the weekly faculty colloquium of St. Andrew's Orthodox Theological School, and so she made this question the theme of her words.

The icon, she said, is often explained as being a sort of book for the illiterate where they may see the persons and stories of that Bible they are unable to read. But as St. Paul says, prophecy and vision are one of the gifts of the Spirit and iconography is grounded in the gift of prophecy to the Church, a grounding which prevents the artist's work from being a mechanical task. All icons are spiritual prophetic visions of the events and figures, and extend the sense of the event. So, for example, the icon of the Assumption (Dormition in the East) of the Virgin Mary, which shows Christ holding his Mother's soul, prophetically extends our understanding of Mary's passing beyond what is in Scripture. Where the gift of prophecy is lost it becomes merely at best an art object. Where, as Fr Zenon Teodor (generally recognized as the greatest living iconographer) says, if the icon is not rooted in worship it can distort faith as surely as theology not rooted in prayer can do. So, late icons of the Trinity show the Father as an old man with a gray beard. What a trivialization and falling away from the prophetic vision of Rublev's Trinity, which, Yazikova says, can no more be described with words than the sea can be drained with a spoon. Furthermore icons prophesy the coming Deification of humanity in Christ; as John says:

It does not yet appear what we shall be.

Now modern Charismatics of the Pentecostal stream often emphasize mostly the gift of tongues, but icons also are a type of charism. The dark glass of Corinthians is washed clear by the Spirit and a window opened to another world or indeed into our own world. So without devaluing or seeking to quench the other charisms, the icon also is a most important Gift of the Spirit as visual expression of the Gift of Prophecy.

The icon as seen in its decadent mechanical phase of mere form, is most inaccessible to Christians outside the Orthodox tradition, and is not much good to those within it either. But in its original and prophetic form it is open, and revelatory, to all.

Walking out of the lecture hall I see the early autumn sun on the sidewalk and then, looking up, its proximate source of reflection—a blazing Glory of radiance on the side of the church roof, a flickering pool of light. How wonderful that the same light, or a higher, may prophetically radiate from the gold flashes of an icon of the Transfiguration or become, in Giotto or Piero Della Francesca, a ground of Splendor.

•

But if there is a distinction between the prophetic and the formal in painting, that distinction rests on the degree in which the painter realizes in himself the presence of the Holy Spirit. This leads to further questions, perhaps by no means simple, such as— what *is* the 'Baptism of the Holy Spirit?'

In *Acts*, Paul asks

> Have you received the Holy Spirit since you believed?

and the people answer that they have not even heard of the Holy Spirit.

Perhaps for many Christians today the situation is not so very different. Of course everyone has, in a literal sense, heard of the Holy Spirit but as far as personal experience many would be able to say only that they have been baptized and confirmed (or chrismated in the East). Of course the Sacrament of Confirmation (Chrismation) represents, and in a deep sense, as we believe, *is* the giving of the Holy Spirit, but the problem is that now that sacramental action is almost always separated from any personal experience... so much so, that any apparent personal realization of the Gifts of the Spirit (such as *Acts* speaks of again and again) would in many places be regarded as disorderly and appalling.

Why this change, so that now usually the most we can say is that the Sacrament gives, as it were, the potential for every gift, is not a simple question...or even when the change took place. For Killian McDonnell of St John's believes, and has assembled such evidence as he finds to the point, that the gifts continued to accompany the administration of the sacrament deep into the patristic period of the early Church.

Whether or not we find his work convincing, it is clear that early or late something changed. And we would suggest that the difference is that in *Acts* it was always a personal act: an Apostle lays hands on a new believer. But as time went by it became less personal and more merely a ritual to be read from a book. But the Spirit is always and only personal...and flows only through and between persons. So valid and right though the administration of the sacrament is, it awaits to be awakened into conscious and personal experience.

If the experience of the Holy Spirit is really personal, then it must be unique in each person.

That is important because the Pentecostal gifts can be expected in a way which is also ritualized and impersonalized as much in a Pentecostal church by a pattern of behavior miming the action of the Spirit as in a Confessional Church where no place is left for any overt action and gift.

If all are different, yet one thing must be in Common: that "Where the Spirit of the Lord is there is liberty" [I Cor. 3:17]. The coming of the Holy Spirit is an experience of being inwardly free—free from all the compulsive plans and fears and thoughts which are centered on ourselves, or rather on our imaginary selves, and which form the medium through which we normally experience and recognize ourselves.

> Inner freedom is the absolute condition of the knowledge of God,

said Maximus, in a phrase whose source I confess to not know—I saw it on a scroll in his hand in an icon (surely a prophetic one) in a seminary classroom. This freedom enables us to step outside of ourselves and into a new and real life. Love, as Maximus also says (and develops in his *Centuries*), is always a going outside of oneself, and so freedom is the beginning of love...and love also is the way of freedom.

For many people, perhaps almost for everyone, this experience of inner freedom is given first in a specific time and then may be deepened in other specific moments. Of course it is possible to not allow oneself to recognize the importance of such a moment, and then it fades like a half-remembered dream: the road in life not taken; 'The hour of one's visitation,' missed, as the Lord says of Jerusalem; or in James, the state of the man who looks into a glass and sees something for an instant, but then forgets.

The German mystics, for example Jacob Boehme and the author of *Theologia Germanica*, loved the terminology of 'new birth' for this , and it is not a bad expression (though it risks being confused with the evangelical term, 'born again' which carries a rather different freight of meaning) of what the Baptism of the Spirit is, because it is a real birth of new life.

Now when a baby is born it gives a little cry of birth and often something like what is called 'speaking in tongues' takes place. It is a rediscovery of sound from its very sources and as a child will learn 'ma' and 'da' and so on, so the newly Spirit-filled person discovers language as something to dare to offer to God as newly coined...or he may even feel impelled (not *compelled*, for tongues is a voluntary action of allowing oneself to string together sounds and offer them to God as the beginning of prayer) —impelled inwardly to do so and to, if we may so say, play with sound as a child does...full of a sense of Wonder. Now what we describe in this way, another might describe as "stringing together nonsense syllables," which is true enough, except that it omits to evaluate that the gift lies in the freedom which dares to do this and offer it to the Creator of the Universe, a real freedom and daring indeed! And on the other hand Charismatics, and perhaps the more Pentecostals, shy away from the radical admission and claim of this understanding, and it is unfortunate because it leads on the one hand to the mystification, and on the other, to the rejection of the experience.

Now, also the process of verbal play which produces prayer in tongues may take place at, or draw from, various levels of the mind and may indeed be free of conscious operation and verge on the purely ecstatic, but we have stated the matter as simply as possible in order to clear away, in as far as possible, the fog which normally surrounds discussion of speaking in tongues.

The gift of tongues may well continue through life as a way of praying, of intercession and of expression of things which are beyond words, but it begins as a gateway of new life, as something very simple, and so it remains. So St. Paul lists it almost as least of the gifts, for it is a beginning one and represents the wonderful experience of the infant, the perpetual beginner.

But for many others this moment of freedom may manifest in other ways which are not less. For one perhaps in a flood of tears perhaps held back for very long. Indeed for St. Symeon, one of only three men (with Gregory Nazianzus and John the Evangelist) formally called 'Theologian' in the East, the gift of tears was a sort of criterion of life in the Spirit, almost as tongues may be for the Pentecostal of today. So St. Symeon says that he cannot see how anyone can worthily receive communion unless he approach it in tears.

But yet for another it may be different again, and manifest in that person as a sense of inner light and of clarity of purpose and an unwonted calm. We stopped longer on Tongues because it is very much the less understood, not because it is greater.

What remains in common to all is the condition of inner freedom, and this freedom itself is the Gift variously shining out in each person. And the more so as we do not limit our expectation, this is how it will be, but present ourselves as truly open to every consequence of freedom.

So we can understand how it is, as is often remarked and objected, that Charismatics and Pentecostals,

'Spirit-filled' people though they be and feel themselves, can be very self-centered indeed. Surely this happens when the beginning is mistaken for the end. That baptizing moment of freedom is meant to be but a beginning of life...We cannot rest in that moment.

The Baptism of the Spirit can be said, as a Dutch writer puts it, to be 'pre-mystical.' The inward way of growth in God and of life in Christ, of which all the spiritual writers and masters speak, comes after that.

And secondly, the Gifts are not possessions. If we hold on to them they will become just manifestations of ego, the Tongues but an ugly personal display and not the original and pure discovery of play with sound before God. At best among many Pentecostals it seems that the exercise of the gift of tongues yearns back towards that one-time freedom, rather than to be a new and renewed experience of it. This is the problem of the Israelites who found that the bread from heaven could not be preserved from day to day. Each day they had to present empty and open hands to receive that day's gift. And of course this need for constant renewal applies to all the gifts we have, really all gifts of the Spirit when understood deeply, for the preacher or teacher or counselor or artist or writer, may find himself repeating what he has said or drawn or written before and doing so with ever decreasing sense of purpose and elan.

Holiness is a flickering flame which passes through and illumines each of us. It is not our possession.

The Creative work of God is a great river of light flowing down from Eternity, from the Eden above and to and through us...

Always *through*. That is so important, isn't it? We cannot dam it up and try to make ourselves a little personal supply. Still less can we think to bottle it and sell it. It is passing through us for the sake of others as through them for our sake and it is only as we let go and give to others that again there is a space for God to enter as He wishes, again and always.

How wonderful when we enter the flow of the Spirit!

> The river of God sets my feet to dancing
> the river of God makes my heart sing...

as a simple hymn goes, and

> The river is flowing...the river is here.

Always here, and everywhere, always now...

These thoughts perhaps from reflections in that pool of Glory and Light on the roof-side on an autumn day. And that this river of light, which is both water and fire, is always personal. and it remains only to pray...

Let the Fire Fall!

On each personally, the same flame manifest so wonderfully differently as God works in each heart.

No gift a personal treasure or toy but so much better than that…it is for others…for service and for Life…our life…always beginning and, no, never ending.

It is 'from Glory to Glory' the life of God Himself in us.

12

THEOSIS

Through the sea...rushed the act of Galahad
He glowed white, leaned against the wind
Down the curved road among the topless waters...
The sole speech was speed...
In a path of lineal necessity,
The necessity of being was communicated
to the son of Lancelot.
The ship and the song drove on.

CHARLES WILLIAMS, *THE LAST VOYAGE*

Williams here, in one of the poems of his remarkable *Arthuriad,* does what scarcely any other Christian poet or, indeed, theologian has dared do; that is, to speak of Divinity, 'necessity of being' is but a philosopher's term for that, being communicated to a mortal man.

But if the poet leaps over and beyond every question of how, even conceivably, a human can share the essence of the Divine life, nonetheless it is possible to find a tradition of reflection in Christianity which works with the question of human Deification and that tradition is related to the word Theosis.

Theosis, a word which may be translated as 'divinization' or 'deification,' is an idea which is beloved of many of the Eastern Orthodox Fathers. Indeed it is often said to be at the heart of what is distinctive in Eastern Christian thought.

It is not an easy concept to grasp. Jaroslav Pelikan has said that the clarification of this concept

> in language that is intelligible to more than a few initiated specialists, is a supreme need for the interpretation of the Eastern Christian tradition to our time.

A first problem is that in its very sound, deification, or even Theosis (if we employ it as an English word as we do, say, 'troika' or 'vodka') is suggestive of pantheism. Of course this rather illicit fragrance is what is also being used as an attraction when it is suggested that Theosis is unique to the Eastern tradition, but then on closer approach any inquirer drawn by the promise of becoming 'one with everything' will be told it is not that at all...Well, but what is it? Can we attempt the clarification that Dr. Pelikan reasonably asks?

Now, as we said it is not a simple matter. We shall have to advance step by step, and even then, when we have presented the basic thought of the theologians as clearly as possible, it may be that there may remain something unsatisfactory and we shall have to see if there is a way we can strike out from there and go on even in a trackless place...perhaps not unlike the sea over which Galahad's ship rushes...However, one step at a time.

First of all there are a number of Biblical expressions which speak of humanity in terms of deification. Psalm 82:6 says,

> Ye are gods, and all of you are children of the most high...

although it also goes on:

> But ye shall die like men.

Jesus picks up the expression in John 10:34-35 in answering criticism that he, a man, made himself God:

> Is it not written in your law, I said, ye are gods?

Then in the First Epistle of John we have this :

> Beloved now are we the sons of God and it does not yet appear what we shall be but we know that when he shall appear we shall be like him, for we shall see him as he is...

II Peter adds the promise that we

> may be partakers of the divine nature.

To this we may add as scriptural background, the expression of Romans that Christ is

> the firstborn of many brethren.

And II Corinthians 3:18,

> but we all with open face beholding as in a glass the glory of the Lord are changed into the same image from glory to glory...

To this also let us add as a starting point of Christian reflection on these things the famous words of St. Athanasius (in *On The Incarnation)* that

God became man so that man might become God,

and the expression is here quite clearly 'become God,' and not 'become God-like.'

So to start with, from these texts, the process of Theosis centers on Christ. Gerard Manley Hopkins puts it very well, and reminds us that we are discussing a matter of more than Eastern Christian scope, in saying:

...in a flash, at a trumpet crash,
I am all at once what Christ is
Since he was what I am, and
This Jack, joke, poor potsherd, matchwood, immortal
        diamond
Is immortal diamond.

St. Maximus says,

In the same way in which the soul and body are united, God should become accessible for participation by the soul and, through the soul's intermediary by the body, in order that the soul might receive unchanging character, and the body immortality and finally that the whole man, soul and body by nature, become God by Grace.

However, we should note at this point that the Eastern Fathers in general speak from a tradition that made a distinction between the essence of God, which is unknowable, and the 'energies' of God—one might say, the acts and revelations of God through which He is known. St. Gregory Palamas—and he so sums up this tradition that today the distinction of essence and manifestation or 'energy' is known as Palamism—says,

> We participate in the nature of God, in His energies, and yet He remains totally inaccessible.

So, although deified, humanity remains humanity, and as St. Macarius says,

> Peter is Peter and Paul is Paul...each one retains his own individual nature but all are filled with the Spirit.

So the exact meaning of Theosis is not so easy to put in a word. We start with Christ who, as the Eastern Christmas prayer said,

> made divine our earthly nature through participation in it.

And as God is always Personal we have the persistence of persons in the all-unity of the deified world. Hegel's idea that increased unity among persons always means increased individuation goes along with the Orthodox Christian approach; the other possibility of course would be the submersion of individuality in all-unity.

Now, one aspect of participating in God in this way and as the Eastern Fathers tend to see it, is that it is not a static state (forever playing a harp on a cloud as in the cartoon image of heaven) but an eternal progression. The point is that God is infinitely inaccessible to the creature who nonetheless is infinitely and eternally moving towards Him and therefore Theosis is an eternal progression. Gregory of Nyssa puts it:

> For those rising in perfection, the limit of the good that is attained becomes the beginning of the discovery of higher goods. Thus we never stop rising, moving from one new beginning to the next.

Certainly, as compared to the cartoon saints playing the harp, this has the quality of stirring the elan and for this, even were it to be incomplete, it shows itself to be a worthy and 'likely account' (as Plato called his myths). It also has the absolutely Christian quality of putting love in the center, for it is, for Gregory and Maximus, love which causes the soul continually to transcend itself (this is the meaning of *ek-stasis*, going outside of oneself in ecstasy, a meaning ecstatically continuing ever on towards the horizon of the Divinity). So Maximus' *Centuries on Love* is, like Gregory's *Life of Moses*, an account of the ascent of the soul, and Theosis is seen as a continual ascent empowered by Love.

Before returning to evaluate this, as we must do, let us first step back and add that Theosis is also, what all spirituality, or at least all Christian spirituality, is: the Mystery of Presence; and therefore it is sacramental and also realized in the Eucharist. Nicholas Cabasilas says:

> In the Eucharist we attain God Himself and God Himself is made one with us in the most perfect of possible unions. This is the final mystery beyond which it is not possible to go, nor can anything be added to it.

And as grounded in Love, Theosis is not only individual but that of the whole humanity and ideally of the whole universe...which as St. Paul says,

> awaits the manifestation of the Sons of God.

The Transfiguration of Christ is mirrored in the transfiguration, Theosis, of the individual who participates in the light of Mount Tabor (as Gregory Palamas loved to say), and also this Light, the uncreated 'energy' of Palamas, transfigures and will yet fully transfigure the Cosmos.

Now this, if in somewhat sketchy outline, is the account of the thought of Fathers like Saints Maximus and Gregory Palamas, and this is usually taken as a good stopping place for discussion of Theosis. 'Beyond this it is not possible to go...' as Cabasilas said.

However, some may find the idea of eternal progression as a terminus, perhaps more satisfactory than strumming a harp on a cloud, but nevertheless, not entirely pleasing. Well of course it is not intended to be like Sisyphus doomed to forever roll a rock up a hill whose top he will never reach, yet is there not, just taken in itself, a bit of that resonance? This was also the thought of the monk Evagrius, who criticizes the idea of eternal progression on the ground that there is no need to go anywhere, as the purified mind reflects God in simple light. St Paul said, after all, that

> Now we see as in a dark mirror but then we shall know just as we are known and see as face to face.

In other words in returning to its own nature the mind discovers itself already in God.

So instead of the 'likely story' about progressing ever forward, we have the account, opposite and yet in its way as stirring to the elan, of waking up and finding oneself already there. The Japanese pilgrim hymn put it,

> A far far distant land is paradise
> I've heard them say
> But those who want to go
> Can get there in a day!

Or as the early Christian Hymn of the Pearl (from the *Acts of Thomas*) expresses it, the soul after a weary journey returns to its Father's house and there it sees:

> My robe of glory which I had put off...its splendour I had forgotten...as I now beheld the robe it seemed to me suddenly to become a mirror image of myself: myself entire I saw in it and it entire I saw in myself...and the image of the King of Kings was depicted all over it...and with its regal movements it pours itself wholly out to me...clothed therein I attained to the Gate of Adoration.

71

Or consider a myth which moves rather in this direction, although of modern rather than Patristic origin, in which C.S. Lewis visualizes:

> a great assembly of gigantic forms all motionless, all in deepest silence, standing forever around a little silver table and looking upon it and on the table were little silver figures like chessmen who went to and fro doing this and that. And I knew that each chessman was the 'idolum' or puppet representative of some one of the great presences that stood by. And the acts and motions of each chessman were a moving portrait, a mimicry or pantomine, which delineated the inmost nature of its gigantic master. And these chessmen are men and women as they appear to themselves and to one another in the world. And the silver table is Time. And those who stand and watch are the immortal souls of those same men and women...Then vertigo and terror seized me...

—'me' being a fictional persona of Lewis...but well might vertigo seize him, for this 'likely story' if you think about it, indeed is rather vertiginous in its implication.

So we have two 'likely accounts' which are apparently mutually exclusive and yet foster the elan in ways which seem about equally necessary—both desirable to the spirit's innermost yearning, and necessary to the Christian tradition in relation to Theosis.

In brief, it would appear that the essential point of eternal progress is that God's creation, and what we see in Jesus, is not simply a cyclic opening up and infolding but something different...an endless opening out. 'Behold, I make all things new!' says Jesus as the Alpha and Omega of the Apocalypse, a thought which the literary modernists of this century could but echo in the dictum 'Make it new!' The Ascending Christ, to put it in another image, breaks through the *Ouroborous*, the worm devouring its own tail (the myth of eternal return, and so on). And what is essential to elan, which is to say yearning, which is to say love, here is the perpetual newness.

Yet again there is also a profound resonance of spirit, is there not, to the idea of waking up?

> In my end is my beginning...the end of all our exploring will be to arrive where we started and know the place for the first time...and all shall be well and all manner of things shall be well when the tongues of flame are infolded into the crowned knot of fire and the fire and the rose are one...

Carol Zaleski, in discussing the comparable problem of finding images for life after death and that the images we do find tend to be contradictory, says, as it seems to me wisely:

> All of these images are needed. None of them is sufficient or exact.

We would suggest then that these two principles, ever-newness and awaking to what has always been there, are the two sides to the understanding of

Theosis; sides which cannot in any way be finally reconciled on the level of 'systematic theology' but which require to be held in mind as two poles that may be reconciled at a higher level. In Hebrew this level is called *Daath*—literally 'knowledge' but knowledge as the creative union of opposites. In some way we might call it 'intuition' but perhaps 'integration' gives a yet higher and deeper sense. May we not perhaps read this need for integration into the words of *Proverbs* that the house of Wisdom is built upon seven pillars? In any case here we may say we have reached a point 'beyond which it is not possible to go,' at least by discursive reasoning... There remain, however, perhaps ways for the mind to go forward even where the paths of reason come to an end...

First, it remains possible to tell more 'likely accounts' as material for integration by some further and higher and deeper operation of mind...So Plotinus:

> There is the soul's peace, outside of evil...all life apart is but a shadow, a mimicry. Life in the Supreme is the native activity of the intellect...this state is its first and its final because from God it comes and its good lies there and once turned to God it is what it was...we have all the vision that may be of Him and of ourselves...but of a self wrought to splendour, brimmed with light, become that light, pure, buoyant, unburdened, raised to Godhood or... knowing its Godhood all aflame then..this is the life of gods and of the godlike and blessed among men.

And Dante, visualizing all the universe as a single rose:

> In that abyss I saw how Love held bound into a single volume all those leaves whose flight is scattered through all the universe around...how substance, accident and mode unite fused together to speak in such wise that this I tell of is one simple light..everything the will has ever sought is gathered there and there is every quest made perfect which apart from it falls short...so strove I with that wonder...high fantasy lost power and here broke off, yet as a wheel moves smoothly free from jars, my will and desire were turned by love,the love that moves the sun and the other stars.

And Dostoevsky has Alyosha, at Fr Zosima's funeral, in reverie see the wedding feast of Cana, at which Jesus turned water into wine, open out to include countless guests at the center of whom, shining like the sun, is the Master:

> He became like one of us from love and he makes merry, turns water into wine, so as not to cut short the gladness of the guests...he is expecting new guests, he is calling new ones unceasingly and for ever and ever...

But beyond the myth, the 'likely story,' there are certain images which seem to arise at a point where the mind has come to an end of words, from a place beyond all merely verbal imagination. Perhaps one is that very Wisdom whose house is supported by seven pillars, and who is, or becomes identified with, that eternal feminine which, Goethe says, leads us on. Another is that very Grail which, in seeking, the High Prince Galahad speeds across uncharted waters... 'No words here,' as Williams says in the poem with which we began this reflection, but yet, drawn by Grail, 'the ship and the song drove on.'

So also we are drawn by these somehow immortal images which we meet at the point where our thought of Theosis reaches its limit, and we now must go what little way we can in following into their mystery.

13

WISDOM

SOPHIA, THE WISDOM OF GOD, is a word coming into rather common use now, but its meaning is not always clear. I asked a friend who has translated many writers from the renaissance of Russian philosophy of the late nineteenth century and first half of the twentieth, works of Vladimir Soloviev, Serge Bulgakov and Pavel Florensky, the Russian Sophiologists if you will: "What is Sophia?"

"Sophia is what all men seek," he replied, which is exactly the phrase used of the Holy Grail to be sure, and then after some thought... "Sophia is the blue sky, the azure of it, though usually the sky is gray or even somehow we live as if we prefer the gray sky."

So the young Vladimir Soloviev on a truly gray day when he had been rebuffed by his first sweetheart, suddenly finds all his consciousness suffused with blue, the azure of the sky, and within that aetheric blue he sees or feels that 'eternal womanhood' is, unlike its particular local representative, holding out a flower to him. And the German romantic who called himself Novalis has a character of his dream of a blue flower in which he sees the face of his beloved whom he may meet but has not yet.

On the face of it there is a rather long road from the Wisdom books of the Old Testament to this romantic vision, and yet it may be a road worth traversing if indeed the one leads to the other. It seems that it can be worth travelling both ways in that case, for perhaps many who speak of Sophia now have not made the journey back to the ground of Divine Wisdom, and it may be that there are theologians who have not often looked to the sky or to the blue among flowers.

Though St. Basil of Cappadocia, remembered as a stern man with a princely mien and a liver ailment as well, writes:

> Look how in a meadow
> the same water becomes
> red in one flower, purple in another
> blue in this one, white in that.

And indeed, although this is not the Basil encountered most by Patristics students today, it is the Basil of the whole book Hexameron (six days of creation), full of a sense of wonder and eager joy at all the marvels of the world, the work, in short, with an eye to the azure sky.

Now, in the Wisdom books of the Bible, from *Job* to *Song of Solomon*, or, if you will include the books of a broader canon, the *Wisdom of Solomon* and *Sirach*, there is a range of material from the conventional aphoristic wisdom of which Job complains when they ply him with their platitudes, (and the poet Archibald Macleish suggested in his play *JB* that the stock phrases of Marxist or Freudian today are no better) to the beautiful,

> Three things are too wonderful for me, four I do not understand, the way of the eagle in the sky, the way of a serpent on a rock, the way of a ship in high sea, and the way of a man with a maid...

—to the darkly shimmering,

> God set eternity in the heart.

But the end of all practical wisdom in these books is the revelation of God's inscrutable mystery: 'the fear of the Lord, that is wisdom...' and human wisdom lies in alignment with the personal being of God and His Wisdom.

God's Wisdom is first of all presented as an inner quality of God who is wise and the source of wisdom... 'All wisdom is from God,' says Sirach. Then Wisdom is sometimes personified: 'Wisdom cries in the streets.' And we are told to 'seek her as silver, search for her as hid treasure.' But this is in effect the sort of personification which one uses to speak of the 'Voice of Reason,' and so on. It is done with other attributes of God as well: 'send out thy light and thy truth that they may lead me,' or 'mercy and truth have met together.'

But then in we see in *Proverbs,* chapter eight, a new departure where the personification is not solely in the human perception but, as it were, from the Divine side. Wisdom, feminine, speaks,

> God possessed me as in the beginning of his ways, before his works of old: I was set up from everlasting, from the beginning, before the earth was when there were no primeval waters I was conceived...when he established the heavens I was present...I was by him as a master workman and I was daily his delight exalting always before him, exulting in his habitable earth and my delight was with the sons of men.

And in the *Wisdom of Solomon* we read in chapter seven,

> she is a vapor of the power of God and a certain pure emanation of the almighty God...the brightness of eternal light, and the unspotted mirror of God's majesty, the image of his goodness...being one she can do all things...conveyeth herself into holy souls...maketh friends of God and prophets.

This language seems to be borrowed by the New Testament writers to refer to Christ himself,

> ...being the brightness of his glory and the express image of his person.
>
> HEBREWS 1:3
> ...The image of the invisible God before all things
> COLLOSIANS 1:15

In the later development it is Christ himself who is the Wisdom of God, and so from one point of view the

Wisdom who works with God in creation is a reaching towards what is more fully expressed in the idea of the Word of God by whom and with whom all things were made [JOHN 1].

Certainly also the Hebrew writers did not imagine an actual female being, a personal Wisdom. She is rather from the Divine side what wisdom crying in the streets is from the human side, a personification and a reminder that the Biblical experience of God is so personal that everything we know of God and his attributes, and His Wisdom first of all, can finally most truly be expressed in personal terms.

But, whatever the intention of the writers, these texts planted a seed which was to grow in wild and luxuriant ways in the gardens of gnostics, and Kabbalists, and Sufis and of all the so various knighthood of that romantic spirituality which flourished in various times in Germany (Jacob Boehme), and France (Louis Claude de Saint-Martin, for example) and in England with Jane Lead and in America among the Shakers, and back to Germany with Novalis and Goethe.

Perhaps the most intense development of this reflection on Divine Wisdom is the Russian, and the Russian Sophiologists, for it now becomes a school and a science of sorts that studies and integrates all that had come before. So Bulgakov's *Unfading Light* is a historical tracing of all that development we have covered so quickly in the previous paragraph. And it was in the British Library, studying Shaker and Kabbalistic texts, that Vladimir Soloviev's climactic vision of Sophia begins with her invitation to him to 'Be in Egypt!'

And so he went to Egypt and struck out into the desert a bit and then, set upon by robbers, he is lying on the sand when Wisdom appears to him. This vision is in its way as central to the matter as are the texts from *Proverbs* and the *Wisdom of Solomon* ,

> All that was and is and ever shall be
> my steadfast glance encompassed it all in one.
> The seas and rivers sparkle blue beneath me
> And distant woods and mountains clad in snow...
> I saw it all and all was one fair image...
> Of woman's beauty holding all as one.
> The boundless was within its form enclosed,
> Before me and in me is you alone...

Now, if to one kind of mind this is very clear, to another it must seem eminent nonsense. Yet if this meditation of Wisdom is in some way an appropriate continuation of the Biblical meditation, ought it not be, as we suppose the Bible to be, universal? Let us pass over all questions of the possible validity of esotericism, and see what universal points we can find...for also it is there rather than in the fascinating enough minutiae of Sophiological theory, or the perhaps still more fascinating character of the knights of Sophia such as Biely and Blok with their love of sunsets and fair ladies, it is there in what is most universal that we are likely to find that which draws on where words have come to a halt in considering the question of Theosis, the Deification of persons and of the universe.

A certain universality is however, even speaking of the persons who sought Wisdom in this path, argued by the wonderful portrait, called 'The Philosophes' of Fr. Serge Bulgakov and Fr. Pavel Florensky done by Mikhail Nesterov. Florensky,that modern Renaissance man, scientist priest and in all esthete, indeed looks the 'philosophe' or esthete, rather delicate and poised like an Afghan hound, if one may say so. Bulgakov, the former Marxist and economist , has added to this the gifts of the philosopher and the visionary priest, and he (his dark business suit contrasting with Florensky's cassock) seems a man of rocklike presence and gravity.

But perhaps, or so it seems to me, what the Sophiologists were about can be approached by stepping back and looking for parallels, perhaps parallels somewhat free of the romantic tinge which is both the attraction of Russian and German sophiology and at the same time is that which makes it easy, perhaps too easy, to dismiss out of hand.

There was for example the medieval personification of Nature as a feminine figure, of which the phrase 'Mother Nature' which remains to us, is if anything a hindrance to approach to that truly awesome personification. We meet her in Jean de Meun's *Romance of the Rose* as defender of creation against death and all diminishment and in whom 'God set the inexhaustible fountain of beauty.' In this, by the way, it seems to me we see Wisdom personified as a kind of opposite to what is represented by Satan. In our century however, and not happily, it is perhaps the personification of good which seems the more fantastical and the demonic, more believable and true to the experience of many than theAngelical. Later, in the Elizabethan poet Spenser we have,

> Great Dame Nature, with...gracious majesty...being far greater and more tall of stature than any of the gods or Powers on high...with a face mortal sight cannot endure for its beauty and its terror...as if the Sunne a thousand times did pass nor could be seen but like an image in a glass and beneath whose feet flowers spring to life.
>
> MUTABILITE VII

Perhaps if the demonic and all that disintegrates and fragments and darkens the world seems more real to us than such an image, it is not the reality of the Angelical image which is so much to be called into question as of our own participation in Reality.

So, in any case, we weave into the Romantic image of Sophia , the grave and majestic vision of the Medieval, and to this we may add the same themes in the imageless language of certain philosophers. For the philosophy of John Scotus Eriugena in *De Divisione Naturae* focuses on precisely the theological meditation of the perfect integrated form of nature. And in our time Simeon Frank, whom Zenkovsky in his magisterial *History of Russian Philosophy*, calls the greatest of Russian philosophers, never uses the word Sophia, or speaks of Divine Wisdom, yet all his writing moves towards what he calls the Panunity, and his final summation (in *Reality and Man*) concludes with a quotation from Goethe:

> And all our cares,
> And all our earthly strife,
> Are but a part of God's
> eternal peace.

So we have Sophia-Natura who is a personification, originally Biblical, but with a very complex history of reflection, of created things in their basic and maximum unity and authenticity as recipient of the creative action of God and in unity with that action.

From this sentence, by the way, you see how verbal expression of the idea becomes dense and Bulgakov's books become longer and longer and denser and denser as he struggles to get it right somehow in mere words. Each explanation seems to fall short of that great dome of Hagia Sophia, which he saw floating on a sea of light at the beginning of his summary of Wisdom. But at his death, Sister Joanna Reitlinger saw that his face had become 'a mass of light.'

Rising above words then, or rather I should say coming from a place beyond them, Wisdom is an image, personified as all in the Biblical world is personal, of integration.

Now maximum integration is what Theosis is about and so we have found a correlative of sorts to Theosis, and we might call it, this Mystery of Wisdom, the Mystery of Presence. Presence of God to the Universe and of the Universe to God, two yearnings become one as the two triangles of David's Star superimposed, become a single image.

Certainly the experience of Christian life may be separated from all this terminology, which if illuminating to some, will be less useful or problematic to others, and totally uninteligible to yet others. But taking the Mystery to be Presence, we will agree with Pavel Florensky that all Theosis, which is to say all spiritual experience, starts inevitably with experience of oneself as grounded in Wisdom.

Solomon's word,

> ...a vapor of the Power of God,
> the brightness of Eternal Light.

Or the azure sky, mirrored in the blue of a flower by the path.

14

GRAIL

THERE IS A GREAT DEAL OF LITERATURE, ancient and modern, concerning the Holy Grail, and not all of it is redolent of Wonder. It is possible to have castles, and knights, and dragons and other wonders, and yet for the story to have no sense of depth, of that sense of awe which rises from what Rudolf Otto called the *numinous* and which Elihu, in the *Book of Job* experienced as the trembling of the hairs on his neck as the Holy passed in the night. When you think of it, the same is true for writings about God, the very source of the numinous, that much theological writing is arid and dry. Yet then there is that religious writing which one immediately recognizes as fragrant of the Holy, and so too among the many Grail books there are some which are 'the real thing,' and are charged with Wonder.

Now to attempt in any direct way to give an account of the Holy Grail and its literature and of all who have been drawn by its fascination would be to write another lengthy book joining that great company of Grail books and this must be beyond our purpose. But we have offered the Grail as an image which draws us forward and inward, beckoning to us from some distance and depth beyond the reach of word. So the idea of Theosis, of the Deification of humanity, is at the heart of Christian faith and theology and yet its meditation can only be pursued to a certain point before words fail...and it is here that the Grail appears to offer assistance. Further, in any case, any theology oriented towards Wonder must take account of that most wonderful of images.

What we shall do then is approach the Grail along just one of the labyrinth of paths that open towards it: that leading through the shimmering and mysterious stories of Arthur Machen, a writer (it is perhaps necessary to say since he is so largely and unjustly forgotten) eminent in the first part of this century and more than almost any other in our time a follower of the way of wonder, and whose work is therefore, though modern, the 'real thing' of which we spoke, a living work in a living tradition. We will suggest that such a work can enable us to immediately see the Grail in a way which many pages of explication could not do.

But first we must offer some basic orientation. In barest outline the story is of the Chalice of the Last Supper, entrusted to Joseph of Arimathea who brought it to the west, perhaps in turn entrusting it to a line of Grail Kings, or perhaps he himself was buried with it. Its Quest is announced at a Pentecost gathering of the knights of King Arthur and all depart to seek it (after all, whatever else it may be, it is what all men seek) but only three, Galahad, Perceval, and Bors achieve the quest and Galahad passes from this world, and the Grail is heard of no more.

Anyone drawn to this may delve into the matter and find at any point paths diverging in bewildering directions. We have said that the Grail is a cup, but Von Eschenbach says that it is a stone, Richard Wagner, when he writes his *Parsifal*, harmonizes this by making it a cup cut from a great emerald. But the images and paths of this material shift ever and again like figures in a dream. Indeed in one book, the *Perlesvaus*, it is said that when the knights traversed an area for a second time its landmarks and hazards were changed, so that they might have new adventures.

Indeed we could do worse than to say that the Grail material is a great dream of the inner meaning of the Eucharist. Perhaps as our nightly dreams may correct our daily thought, and the rationalist by day must experience fantasy by night, so the Grail meditation of the medieval authors arose as counterpoise and completion to the rational work of definition of the Eucharist within the Latin Church of that time. By comparison, in the East the mysterial and rational meditation of the Sacrament were not separated, but held together in a single sense of Mystery, and this has theological virtue and yet on the other hand leaves a relative absence of either analysis or dream. It may be a little as in one language a single word will cover what two signify in another tongue, and there are advantages to the understanding in both the unity and the division of nuance.

Now We may go further, and this is as much as we will attempt by way of definition, and suggest that the Grail meditation is first of all that of the Eucharist from the point of view of the cup shared in the Kingdom and after the Resurrection...the Lord having said that he would not eat and drink again until anew in the Kingdom. There is nothing unorthodox about such a meditation but it does bring a new perspective and one distinct in some way from the usual Eucharist of the Church, which is first of all that of the Upper Room looking to the Cross. Not, of course, that the Eucharist can be divided, but its ways of meditation can. So for example Chretien de Troyes finds nothing incongruous in having a woman bearing the Grail (after the Resurrection, St. Maximus and Eriugena said, Christ is not simply male but the full humanity reconciling both sexes) though he would never have imagined a woman celebrating Mass in his parish. It is the Same Mass, yet carried somehow a step further in sacred history.

Secondly, that the Grail represents the continued Presence of Christ within the world, and the cult of Adoration of the Blessed Sacrament, Benediction for example, seems to spring from the atmosphere of the Grail even more than from that of the theologians and schoolmen. In the large sense the Earth itself, which received the falling blood of the Savior, is Grail. So, Fr. Serge Bulgakov can say,

> The Holy Grail abides in the world, as the mysterious holiness of the world, as the power of life...in which the world will be transformed.
>
> THE HOLY GRAIL: EXEGESIS OF JOHN 19:34

And when he was in China, Fr. Teilhard de Chardin shows the spirit of a knight of the Grail, for lacking bread or wine with which to celebrate the Mass, he offers the world itself as matter of the Eucharist, as the sun rises over the Gobi desert on Easter morning.

S.A. Laubenthal wrote only one novel, *Excalibur*, but it is a rather good one which deserves more reading then it gets. In any case she sums up this Cosmic aspect of the Grail (which when you think of it is not separate from its Resurrectional aspect) and does so nicely:

> ...and then he knew that everyone, all the people...gone, living and unborn, stood in some instant of life and death at the place of the Grail...the possible and the impossible, the real, the aspiration, the depth and the height that was what it was, the

> reconciliation of all these, not in an instant of time
> but in all time, everywhere and always the action of
> this reconciliation: that was the true work of God
> and man…and with that, as he answered "Amen" a
> golden light broke from the Grail like the rising of
> the sun.

This is, not only in its Eucharistic vision but in its charging of language with wonder, close to the sprit as well as the sense of the old romances.

Which brings us to Arthur Machen, who has this quality, it seems to me, in preeminent measure. Machen (1867-1947), was a Welshman, a man of letters in the broad sense of essayist, journalist, and reviewer, novelist and tale-spinner. In his time he was admired by contemporaries, from Oscar Wilde to John Betjeman, but I daresay he is not much read today and if, outside a circle of Machenians, he is remembered at all it is probably for his influence in the rather narrow field of 'horror' fiction, where his stories do indeed form a link in the chain from Poe to H.P.Lovecraft, and are as dark and decadent as anything from those masters of the genre.

He was also, for a time, on the edge of the occult and maintained a life-long friendship with the Christian esotericist and prolific author A.E.Waite, whose occult temple Charles Williams and Evelyn Underhill patronized for a time. But Machen's deep and permanent position was that of a high-church

Anglican and of a Celticist—for him that Church seemed closest to the old faith of the British Isles.

His thought and religion, however, arose most of all not from love of place and tradition but from a sense of the limits of knowledge. In the Eastern Church this is the apophatic *(via negativa)* tradition, with which he would have been seen to have a real and deep affinity, if his ideas were laid out as a systematic theology instead of being, as they are, expressed in images. His thought, here, is summed up in the phrase he loved: 'omnes exeunt in mysterium,' all things (considered in their depth) lead into ineluctable mystery. This feeling dovetails perfectly with the mood of mystery of Celtic tradition and of the Welsh mountains and valleys. Arthur Machen was a mystic, but one of a specific sort—not so much a mystic of ecstatic or revelatory experience but a mystic in that he is ever aware of the mystery behind things and people. He regards all with a deep sense of wonder and of the unfathomable.

In his stories of terror, particularly perhaps in the ones in *The Great God Pan* and perhaps still more in *The Three Imposters* which I find a rather...terrible book, he looks into the mystery of darkness. And these are, relatively, remembered, but in his Grail stories he looks into the Light, with I should say a no less unblinking eye.

In *The Great Return* (1915) he tells the story of the coming of the Grail to a Welsh fishing village. It stays only for a time, a time of healing when old enemies become friends, and sickness is made well.

> Old men felt young again, eyes that had been growing dim saw clearly, and saw a world that was like Paradise, the same world it is true, but a world rectified and glowing as if an inner flame shone in all things. Joy and wonder were in all faces...

An old Methodist deacon cries out, what surely hardly another Methodist deacon has cried,

> Priesthood of Melchizadek! Priesthood of Melchizadek! The altar that is of a colour no man can discern is returned, the Cup that came from Syon is returned, the...Three Holy Fishermen are among us and their net is full *Gogoniant, Gogoniant!*—Glory, Glory!

And after the celebration of Mass at the parish church...

> There were a few who saw three come out of the door of the sanctuary, and stand for a moment on the pace before the door. These three were in dyed vesture, red as blood. One stood before two looking to the west, and he rang a bell. And they say that all the birds of the wood, and all the waters of the sea, and all the leaves of the trees, and all the winds of the high rocks uttered their voices with the ringing of the bell. And the second and the third; they turned their faces one to another. The second held up the lost altar once called 'Sapphirus' which was like the changing of the sea and of the sky, and like the admixture of gold and silver. And the third heaved up high over the altar a cup that was red with

burning and with the blood of offering. And the old rector cried aloud then before the entrance: *Bendigeid yr Offeren yn oes oesoedd!* —Blessed be the Offering unto the ages of ages!

And then the Mass of the Sangraal was ended, and then began the passing out of the land of the holy persons and holy things that had returned to it after long years...

We quote at length because this work is not easy to find, but more because the tone seems that of the full tradition of the thing. C.S.Lewis said of George MacDonald that he could write a modern myth as no other man, unless it be Kafka. I would say of Machen that he can breathe wonder into words as no other writer in our time. There is no less wonder in his Grail novel, *The Secret Glory*, but he is really properly a short-story writer, and the plot of the book involving the coming to maturity of a young man at a public school is rickety and awkward. However, all of this is to frame his relation to the Grail, which begins when he is taken by his father to the house of a farmer, a hereditary guardian of the Grail, who has received the 'Cup of St. Teilo,' which the saint had from the Lord in Paradise. They descend into the locked basement and kneel before the cup; the boy Ambrose's father and the man chant an old liturgy in Welsh and as they do he goes into a reverie:

His spirit was lost in the bright depth of the [cup's] crystal, and he saw the ships of the saints without oar or sail, afloat on the faery sea, seeking the glassy isle. All of the whole company of blessed saints of the Isle of Britain sailed on the adventure; dawn and sunset, night and morning their illumined faces never wavered; and Ambrose thought that at last they saw the bright shores in the dying light of a red sun, and there came to their nostrils the scent of the deep apple gardens in Avalon and odours of Paradise.

And as the Liturgy chanted by the two men in pure Welsh continues, the boy's vision moves to its measure,

Then he stood by a wild sea-shore ..a white moon of fourteen days old, appeared for a moment in the rift between two vast black clouds, and the shaft of light showed cliffs that rose up into mountains whose bases were scourged by the hissing foam driven against them by the hollow sounding sea...[and] on the highest ...a great castle and church, and all its windows were ablaze as if every pane were a diamond...And he knew the place was the Sovereign Perpetual Choir, Corarbennic, into whose secret the deadly flesh may scarcely enter. But in the vision he lay breathless on the floor before the gleaming wall of the sanctuary while the shadows of the hierurgy were enacted, and seemed to him that in a moment of time, he saw the Mystery of Mysteries pass veiled before him, and the Image of the Slain and Risen.

The dream was broken and he heard his Father singing softly "Gogoniant y Tad ac y Mab ac yr Yspryd Glan," and the old man answered "Agya Trias eleeson ymas," and again his spirit was lost in the depths...

We have said something of what the Grail may seem to us to be and of how it is an image of Theosis in which God and the world are joined in a single form. We have said that, but Arthur Machen has shown us, and for this alone (though all his work is full of wonderful things) he is a master of Wonder and in our time a knight of the great company of the Grail.

15

TOWER

GALAHAD, HIGH-PRINCE OF SARRAS, looking into the Grail experienced 'wonder on wonder,' and he did not return but passed on beyond the circles of this world. But the others all returned to tell the story of their search, and of whatever, in what measure, they had found.

On the shore of Miyajima in western Japan stands a Torii, a great shrine gate of two red columns joined by a crosspiece at the top. Every shrine has its gate but this is exceptional in that it stands on the beach, and in the water when the tide is in. Its shrine is on a wooded hill behind the beach, as I recall, but what I certainly remember is this great outline of a gate standing there in the edge of the sea. It seems a standing glyph or ideogram, but signifying what? Or a gate, but to where? I am unable to pass through.

Glastonbury is a small town in the west of England, not far from Cornwall and Bath and Bristol. Perhaps its name is remotely derived from Avalon (Arthur's destination beyond death), which might in turn be a transformation of Annwyn, the Celtic land of the dead. There is the legend that Arthur himself was buried here, and St. Patrick, and St. Joseph of Arimathea together with the Grail whose guardian he was. In any case it is no doubt the single place in the world most identifiable with the Holy Grail tradition, and a place around which a complex of myths and legends is woven.

John Cowper Powys, the contemporary Welsh novelist and author of *Glastonbury Romance,* a sprawling novel set in the town early in this century, says through one of the characters of that book,

> There are only about a dozen reservoirs of world magic on the whole face of the globe, Jerusalem... Rome... Mecca... Lhassa—and of these Glastonbury has the largest residue of unused power. Generations of mankind, aeons of past races, have by their concentrated will made Glastonbury miraculous.

In the literal sense of magic one is reminded of a set of stories by the science fiction writer Larry Niven based on the premise that there is a time in the old history of the world when the stock of available magic is so depleted that it becomes more and more difficult for magicians to ply their trade until finally they are supplanted by the iron-age cultures of emerging human history.

That aside, the image is strong and yet in a set with the other places, Glastonbury might easily seem the one that does not belong. After all, those other places each have some clear focus: the Potala, the Kaaba, the Vatican, the Dome of the Rock and Wailing Wall, and furthermore each of them is the center of a whole definable spiritual culture.

The situation is rather different with Glastonbury. It is a town of some 7,000 people or so now, with a few medieval buildings but mostly new and there is a good deal of Woodstock about it with the shops selling trinkets of the 'New Age' and little models of dragons and wizards with pointed caps and such. A bit out of sight, but convenient, behind a hill is a large supermarket in the center of a complex of stores like a gentrified shopping mall in the States. There are a good many hippies and street people coming and going more or less seasonally and the local member of parliament is usually Conservative.

The town is set in the midst of moors which can still flood, and once perhaps were permanently under water and later seasonally flooded. So the name of the area—Somerset—refers to the seasonal rise and fall of the water.

There are perhaps three features of particular note in Glastonbury. There is a spring which brings water apparantly from some depth and distance. This ought not in itself be the basis for more than some local competitor, in a small way, of *Evian* spring water. There are some ruins of the old Abbey at Glastonbury. It was once a great enough Abbey, though as a goal of pilgrimage surely less than Canterbury or York and it is now reduced to a bare outline of ruins and a great green lawn. The ruins are not enough to allow one to visualize the original structure very well and there are many standing Cathedrals, such as the great and wonderful Wells Cathedral not ten miles up the road, similar to, and likely finer than what the Abbey was in its day.

Thirdly, there is the Tor, a hill of rather remarkable shape topped by an old tower, all that remains of a church dedicated to St. Michael. The men of medieval times built churches dedicated to St. Michael on many mountains, perhaps sensing his fitness to be guardian of 'high places' which can, as the Tor in legend is, also be portals to the underworld and the land of the dead or of faerie. The Tor is an odd and rather fey place but it can hardly be among the most romantic or striking hills of the world.

James P. Carley, author of a very fine history centered on the Abbey, *The Holy House at the End of the Moor Adventurous*, remarks that if the little lad who observed that the Emperor had no clothes were to go to Glastonbury he would know just what to say, and yet

> perhaps the child rather than being heroically honest was needlessly destructive...Does his success in destruction make his judgment admirable, or even correct?

In any case, Glastonbury, whether or not for any reason deeper than its history and the accretion of legends and people attracted to them, is deeply associated with the Grail matter and is of a piece with that matter in refusing to be pinned down or defined by any isolated concreteness.

Concerning the Tor, Geoffrey Ashe, a journalist from Toronto who came to Glastonbury to stay and become a noted Arthurian scholar, says:

> The landscape is weird yet the essence of its weirdness is hard to catch. A green quilted acreage of reclaimed marsh stretches away and away...in the center, visible at great distance and at queer angles, a skewed cone five hundred feet in height shatters the skyline. This is Glastonbury Tor... optically speaking the landscape does not makes sense. It is a monstrous refraction. The Tor so obvious for many miles vanishes in the town and hides behind objects too small to conceal it. Although a natural formation, it soars in terraces like a Mexican pyramid. A church tower which surely ought to be below displays itself on the summit, but without any church...

My own experience with this aspect of it centered on a peculiar sense of distance. The tower towards which I climbed, through fields, past grazing sheep, over a wicket and then up a hill, seemed extremely distant and, as it were, at the far horizon until suddenly what had been set in the horizon a moment before was right there. Often a poet or novelist will state a thing best, and Flann O'Brien in *The Third Policeman* writes of a truly queer building which hardly seems to belong in this spatial dimension,

> The whole morning and the whole world seemed to have no purpose at all save to give it magnitude and frame it so that I could find it with my simple senses and pretend to myself that I understood it.

This was my experience, people experience it differently, and at least for those susceptible to suggestion of the magical it is a fairly queer place.

I am on another hill, Jasna Gora (*Lookout Mountain*) in Poland at night, a Sister is guiding me towards the lodge which is at the top when suddenly all over the hill the electric power goes out...we are suddenly disoriented and, until our eyes begin to adjust, in absolute darkness, but we continue forward in that darkness. "Now," she says, "you are a real pilgrim."

On Christmas Eve in the little town of Nakanida a farmer named Jonah Kumagai comes walking to Vespers down a long road, which his sons traverse by car. It happens every year at Christmas. He has no special knowledge of the faith, I think, or of the ways of pilgrims but, Father Yamaguchi says, he wishes on this day 'to be a pilgrim.'

In another night, over vodka, the talk turns to spiritual darkness. A Dutch pastor says, "I do not have much experience of that , but I only know that often in the night I pray until the darkness comes and I can pray no more." We pray and as we voice our prayers he provides an undertone of humming and clicking, which I suppose to be his 'tongue,' deep and unearthly, unless it be like some aboriginal instrument, but full of power and peace.

In a night in New York, a Passover night, Rebbe Dovid is at table, and here are his few Hassids, Mordechai and Yehuda and some other friends, and he begins a *niggun*, a wordless melody...

Not long after that, on the anniversary of the destruction of the Temple he will be fasting in Israel and an Israeli soldier will have to break his teeth with a rifle butt to force nutriment into his emaciated body and save him. And not long after that, at Notre Dame in South Bend, he will die of heart failure.

And my mother after long endurance of the asphyxia (which was the way of the Cross) of congested lungs, endurance without indulgence in self pity, says that "God will keep us...and especially you," and a little later, "God help me..." and she dies.

Al Nur looks into my eyes and reads "some gift from suffering..." He is not old, but he will die suddenly within a year of cancer. He strikes the drum with his palm, and his eyes become distant..."I am a lover of the lovers of God."

Now it is Dovid who strikes the table and picks up the melody...*Lei la la lei la la lei la la! Lei la Lei la lei la la!* And on...His voice and the melody annihilate time.

...at dawn in a small boat out of an island off east Japan, with Marc and Sylvain of Taizé, meeting the fishing fleet...mist...seagulls...a world of new born light.

And now it is day...high above the land stretched like a map in every direction of the compass and I enter the tower, through one of its facing arched doors. Looking up I see the sky, for the tower now has no roof and the clouds pass above. In this way it seems an image of the Church for our time and the time to come, its stone rooted firmly in the earth and stretching to the sky but now open to the wind, to the movement of the Spirit who is the Church's Lord. I step through the tower and out the other side and walk around it once and again. Is this, the Tower as image of the Church which is to be, what I have found at the end and that with which I will return to tell the tale, if not in Camelot then to a few graduate students and some others?

I stand back and look again at the Tower and its facing doors.

Karina has attended a presentation I gave on the Grail at a faculty colloquium of St Andrew's Orthodox School of Advanced Biblical Studies in Moscow. In the afternoon she sleeps a little and dreams near waking of a great Chalice which she understands somehow to be the place where opposites are reconciled. Is this cup marriage? Yes it is that...but also it is more. "Perhaps, it seemed to me, the Grail is Community where all the opposites are reconciled."

The superimposed doors of the two sides of St. Michael's are a gate. I go through.

16

COMMUNITY

I FIRST BECAME ACQUAINTED WITH Fr. Alexander Men, the great modern priest-teacher and almost final martyr of the communist period, through photographs shown me by Jim Nichols, a psychotherapist and photographer from San Francisco. The photographs were taken at Fr. Men's house in Semhoz, a little hamlet outside Moscow where he had lived in the years before his death in 1990. In 1992 Jim and his wife were with a tour group in Zagorsk, the famous Russian monastery town. They had a bit of free time and at the suggestion of Joan Ashton, an English author who knew something of Alexander Men and remembered that his house was nearby, they set off in search of Semhoz. It seemed a doubtful proposition, given the language problem, but the taxi-driver they found happened to be the brother of the police officer who had first investigated Fr Men's murder, and who was therefore able to take them to the location, a small group of wood cottages in the forest. The house itself was, and is, surprisingly large (having been extended), a wooden summer house in the midst of a fenced garden. It is orderly within (unlike some Russian homes where, as someone has said, the owners appear to be camping out in their own homes; or on the other hand without the sense of sterility of some American homes) and it is, if one may so put it, a peaceful orderliness.

What touched the visitors that day, and touched them very deeply, was the warmth with which Fr. Men's wife, Natasha, and the family, greeted them and showed them everything. After all they were only tourists, and the Men family were people of the world who surely must have had more than enough visitors interested in Fr. Alexander.

It was shortly after this that I saw the photographs Jim took: here a number of photos of the library, the bust of Dante, the menorah, the icon corner, some of the books, showing at close inspection many in English (Dodd on the Fourth Gospel, Peter Brown of Princeton and others) evincing a wide-ranging mind and sympathy. Here is the family. And here is the place where Fr. Alexander was struck down. The glade is bright and green and somehow bathed in an amazing light. I sensed that here was something special...

We have spoken of 'thin' places where the veil or line between this world and the world of the Divine seems to become thin or even disappear. Although , as with Glastonbury, this generally relates to a some-what mystical conception of accumulated sanctity and of place. There is that at Semhoz of course, the past somehow still present. Not only is it the place of Fr. Men's life and martyrdom, but it is at the center of that ancient heart of Russia where St. Sergius of Radonezh and the miraculous iconographer St. Andrey Rublev lived. Indeed it may very well be that St. Sergius, six hundred years before, walked the same path which Fr. Men took daily through the wood to the bus-stop where he was finally assassinated.

So there is history at Semhoz, but I wonder if also Christian hospitality and lived faith, such as that which my friends experienced from the Men family, does not also render a place 'thin?' If so of course we may come upon (or dare we hope also to create?) thin places unsuspected by connoisseurs of sacred sites. In any case the specialness one felt looking at those photographs was surely that of holiness...

The forest was radiant with the same light which I had felt in those photographs on the eve of Pentecost in 1995, when, at the invitation of Natasha Men, I was there on retreat with some twenty people of a small Orthodox lay Community devoted to prayer and mission to youth.

I remember that day as a day of amazing light and color, the blue sky, the green forest stretching away and away, the yellow and white flowers, and the water running on the forest floor. The wind was very strong and yet unharming. It seemed a day outside the natural order, a day belonging to some other level of reality, whose colors were purer and more vivid than those of the world I knew.

I had come to identify with and to love these, mostly young, people and when we gathered in the library I shared with them some thought...

•

"When the day of Pentecost had fully come they were all with one accord in one place."

Surely the words "with one accord" open for us the deep mystery of Community. So the Lord said, "if two of you shall agree on any thing they shall ask it shall be done." And then immediately the parallel words : "for where two or three are gathered together in my name there am I in the midst of them." The Lord is saying that in agreement, in the being together of two or more, a new condition is created which makes it possible for Him to act and be present in a way in which he could not otherwise act or be present. This new condition is precisely Community, and Community is revealed and fulfilled most perfectly on the Day of Pentecost where the disciples gathered "with one accord."

Now I think that the Mystery of Community is very deep and is finally none other than that of the Church herself, and that it is only beginning to be meditated upon and disclosed within the history of the Church. So Fr. Men loved to say that the Church has only begun to realize and to disclose her inner reality, that the Church is like an arrow well-launched, but only beginning its course, or like an infant yet. And that in which the Church is yet developing is most of all in this which is most inward to it, and yet most difficult...for consider that in no other religion is there anything really comparable to the Church in this aspiration to make one Body of many members.

So anyway, we start from the question: What is the agreement, the 'of one accord' of answered prayer and of Pentecost?

Now, we may begin with the consideration that if agreement is important, then both persons, or all persons, agreeing are valuable and important. Agreement is not necessary except between equal persons. If one is important and not the other then no agreement is necessary, so the basis of community and of the coming of the Holy Spirit is the dignity of all persons. This is what the Lord Jesus is finally able to tell his disciples for the first time at the Last Supper, isn't it? "Henceforth I call you not servants but friends." He is offering them through the promised coming of the Holy Spirit a new intimacy which is expressed in the agreement of friends. Thomas Merton in a lecture given on the day of his death uses the expression: "from now on brother, every man stands on his own feet." Again in these remarkable words is expressed the realization of the unique creativity and value of each person and of how it is Community (expressed by 'brother' as the Lord says 'friends') in which this is possible. This is one gift of the Spirit: the gift of ourselves.

So the agreement of two or more in community opens the mystery of persons, but also then there is the mystery of how two can agree. If there are two must there not be a contradiction? Here the Lord at that same Supper gives the new commandment which is the commandment of Pentecostal agreement: "A new commandment I give you, that you love one another." And He shows that commandment in the washing of the disciples' feet, emphasizing its total importance and saying that only in the future will they begin to understand what He has done and shown them.

"What I do you know not now, but you shall know hereafter." Beyond the mystery of persons then there is the Mystery of agreement of persons, the being together and working together and breathing together as one of free persons. The possibility of oneness, of agreement, is the second gift of the Spirit revealed in Community. Indeed it can only be revealed in Community! Its law is sharing and exchange: "bear one another's burdens. Let each think not of his own (gifts) but of those of the other." And of love and of humility: "let this mind be in you which also was in Christ Jesus. For the Mystery of Community is that of the 'friends' and of the "giving of (one's)life for (one's) friends."

The friends who have given their lives to each other in the Lord, these are the two or three who agree, these are the disciples gathered with one accord at Pentecost. In aspiration at least this is—it must be!—what we are, we and all Christians today in our churches, or in religious communities, or intentional communities, or indeed in whatever grouping of Christians we find ourselves and with which we are given to identify. This being of one accord with those to whom one has given one's life is what Community is, is it not? And so in community one becomes that full person, the friend, the brother (or sister) standing on her (or his) own feet, and at the same time one becomes the friend who gives his life to the others to serve them, and with them to serve the world for Christ. In the discovery of ourselves in Community. Furthermore, the Church also discovers (through us, through the two or three in agreement) more and more the depth of her own meaning. The revelation of the Mystery of Community reveals, and will reveal yet more, the Mystery of the Church...

To the gifts of the Spirit in Community we must add those gifts which the Spirit pours out on each individual in Community. For as one's life is lived with and offered to Community, the gifts of each are for all. This includes those gifts which are apparently natural and already there and which now acquire a new significance. It includes newly revealed gifts. We say 'apparently natural' because everything is from God. So we may think of the ability to learn as a natural gift but as Mikhail Nesterov's amazing painting shows us, St. Sergius receives as a boy the gift of learning from an angel, and so do we receive our 'natural gifts' though most of us do not have Sergius' gift to see or Nesterov's to portray the Angelicals! How many are the wonderful gifts of God! A hymn of the nineteenth-century American sect known as Shakers begins:

It's a gift to be simple. Its a gift to be free...

Indeed! Hardly any gifts could be greater. There are gifts of song, and of joy and of a particular smile...the gift of courage and the gift of peace. The gift of vision of the unseen and the vision of what will be (prophecy) and the gift of vision of what should be...the gift of tears and the gift of laughter. Fire and ecstasy are a gift and so is a radiant calm. Tongues are a gift and so too is the language of science and analysis. The gifts of healing by prayer, the gifts of a faithful doctor. The insight of the elder is a gift and so too of the psychologist. It is a gift to lead for the sake of others; the words *servus servorum dei*—servant of the servants of God, are also fulfilled exactly in those gifted to lead in Community.

Now all these gifts are different but no gift must quench another. No gift must devalue another or make its manifestation impossible. How can this be? Only, again, in the mystery of the agreement of two or three, where each receives and uses his gift only for the others. Padre Pio or St. Francis bore in their bodies the stigmata, the signs of the Passion. St. Seraphim revealed in his body Resurrection light. St. Joseph of Cupertino rose in the air as he prayed the Liturgy. The gifts have no limit or measure beyond the will of the Spirit and of our openness to receive them, for the sake of the others, of the Church, for the Community.

So everything is Gift, is Charism, our unique personhood, our possibility of oneness together, and all our individual gifts received for the sake of the Community.

A gift is not something that we have on our own. Considered in ourselves we are all on the contrary limited and broken and full of impossible contradictions even within ourselves—not to speak of with others. We have no wholeness individually or together, but we have the possibility to receive as a gift that which we could in no way establish ourselves. This too is the meaning of our agreement to seek, for the sake of the others (and for the Lord's own sake) that which we would be unable even to ask for our own sake alone. For the sake of the others we dare to ask for the gift of ourselves, of our humanity as a unique person and friend of the Lord, but it is precisely because we ask it for the others that we may, and will, receive it. May the Lord find us 'gathered with one accord' and 'in agreement' And may he give us with new depth and power the great gifts of Community by his Spirit, and may the Holy Spirit disclose and open out in each of us those individual gifts with which we can serve each other, and together serve Christ in the world! May we in no way limit the Spirit but in every way be open to Him, even as on that day when the Time of Pentecost was fully come, and the disciples were all gathered 'with one accord.'

•

We spoke on that bright Pentecostal day of how the gifts seem to come in paired opposites, it is a gift to be coolly analytical and a gift to be full of joy and ecstasy, and so on.

Beyond that it seems to me that the Community, at least as I have found it, is a way of balance, indeed of a whole series of balances. Balance of the personal and of the communal, of the spiritual and of the practical, including all the concrete circumstances of our lives, family work and so on. Balance of ministry of the word and of social service. Balance of an ever deepening understanding and experience of the Church's Tradition, and of searching for new ways. Balance of taking in and of giving out, of love of the Church and of reaching out to those outside, of silence, and of action grounded in peace.

As with the gifts, it is not a matter, or so it seems to me, of striking a balance or mean between two extremes but of the full expression of apparent opposites in a balanced way, which is possible only in the Holy Spirit who reconciles opposites. As the contemporary Russian philosopher Simeon Frank speaks of the 'hovering knowledge of the dove' which unites antinomies, so it is in a practical way this by which Community lives.

It is precisely that reconciliation which was called the Grail... and who could doubt, on that brightest and clearest of days, that then and in Semhoz that is what it was?

17

UNITY

THERE ARE TIMES WHEN one says a thing without truly and fully knowing it, true though it may be, and then there are times when without speaking one knows.

In a garden in Paris there is a gathering of graduates of an evangelism school known as Jeunesse Lumière, founded by Fr. Daniel-Ange. There are to be some greetings given. Cardinal Schonbron from Vienna speaks. I do not remember all he said, but it was as calm and clear as he is. Then we said a few words on Peter and John in the Temple. May the day come again when Peter and John will again say as they did to the lame man, "look at *us*," not "look at me..." This requires something deeper than formal unity, which could be but a journalistic event, passed of by many with a shrug and a yawn. The yearning and prayer and travail given to the search for unity is not for this. Rather, what is longed for and required is nothing less than a new Pentecost, and a standing together. 'Within the Name of Jesus...' says Peter, and it is a word of power. In our time too let it be spoken... Then, as the Psalmist said,

> Many shall hear! Many shall fear! and many shall trust in the Lord!

All this I believe to be true. But do I know it? To put it another way, desirable as a New Pentecost may be, and granting of course that its form of manifestationwould be beyond our forethought, do we really know, do I really know, do I even really think, that God is preparing in any near future an event as epochal as Pentecost? That the full and apparent Unity of Christ's Church will be manifest and that this union will be sealed by this Sign? Surely what we are speaking of, to have that effect 'that the world may believe,' would have to go far beyond, and probably be very other than, the Charismatic Renewal of the 1960s, by which many of my generation measure their expectation of a 'New Pentecost.' Are we, now allowing Hopkins' 'leaden echo' to sound, not the changeable changed, like some dreamer of 'perpetual revolution' projecting into the future a larger and idealized and triumphant version of the Paris Spring of the 1960s?

On one level, I have no answer. I understand that perhaps I spoke without knowledge (yet true word may leap ahead of knowledge and only the fearful or the pedant will rein word back always to what he knows). Yet in a way I have received, and can offer to you also, knowledge—which I will share if you will come with me on a certain Monday evening to a flat in the south of Moscow.

This is one of the homes where we meet for Bible study and then for prayer... the room is large enough, but now crowded all around with perhaps twenty-five people, pressed against the bookcases which are piled with books. Photographs of Metropolitan Anthony Bloom, of Mother Theresa, of Sister Madelaine of the Little Sisters of Jesus, and icons of the Washing of the Feet, of the Entrance into Jerusalem, and many others, look on from wall or glass case.

Sveta has begun the study with an overview of the section in Romans chapter twelve where Paul speaks of the separation of Israel, the mystery of that separation and of the ultimate reunion. Tamara observes that even now we can pray together for the Parousia, the Second Coming, though they may not with us identify that with Jesus. Andrey suggests that perhaps the union of all must take place first and this reunion be the final accomplishment of the Mystery of reunion. "Can we pray together with them?" someone asks, and answers his own question, "there is no alternative."

The guitar strummed, we sing softly the Niggun,
Yeshuah ha Moshiach, Uadon...Uadon...Levod Elohim.
—Jesus...Messiah! Most High in the Glory...
And then just "Jesu...Jesu..."

Then we pray, passing a candle round the circle of people crowded in the room. Each receiving the candle prays and then passes it on.

I am not so often or easily a patient person, and I have not always felt entirely at ease in this sort of situation. Some crazed mathematician working away in my mind calculates an recalculates the number of people who have prayed, the number who will yet, and the prospective number of remaining minutes of prayer together with the percentage past. But tonight that will change because as the candle is passed around, I begin to think not so much of and as myself, this single restless point of consciousness so divided against itself, but as yet that simply within the circle. And then I have a great feeling of height, of being seen from a great height, and somehow also seeing from that height, and seeing and seen as within, a circle of light.

For, as Boris Pasternak says in the Easter poem of the lights of an Easter procession...'the flames become a track of light...' and so our prayers and passed candle are a perfect circle. There is a vertigo of height as of depth.

The prayers are one prayer, the moving flame and the prayer are One.

The Mystery of Unity in a circle of light falling into Absolute Height... This much I know and can share with you...

In a crowded room on a Monday night.

18

MAGI

LATE ONE NIGHT AS A PRIEST drove me back to the seminary where I was studying, he spoke of his deep concern for his sister's little daughter who was gravely ill. He said, "I have prayed that if necessary the Lord would take me instead of her. I have done most of the things I set out to do...Let it be me." This left me moved, yet feeling there was something wrong. Perhaps it is a too easy assumption that one's work is complete, and that indeed we in this immediate case 'owe God a death' and that we can set the terms of exchange in that case. Yet allowing all this, and whatever more, which may be said, it seemed, and still seems, to me a reaching out towards something very Christian, very true.

Charles Williams, the visionary novelist and poet of the Inklings circle in Oxford, said:

> The doctrine of the Christian Church depends, on the substitution...of our sacred Lord for us. The activity of the Christian Church may need to recover more than is commonly supposed, our substitution one for another.

Williams began a fraternity called The Order of the Coinherence for the purpose of the practice of substituted love. In his novel *Descent into Hell*, he gives us examples of what he has in mind. A writer named Peter Stanhope, learning that Pauline, a new acquaintance, has a terrible fear of meeting her Doppelganger (an exact double of herself) as she has once, offers to bear her fear for her: in effect saying, I will take this on myself and you will be free of it. And so it is. He experiences her fear in himself...

> The burden was inevitably lighter for him than for her, for the rage of a personal resentment was lacking. He endured her sensitiveness but not her sin...

Then later she offers the fear which she endured for long years and the pain of it, in exchange for the fear of an ancestor, some hundreds of years before, who is in terror of the martyrdom by fire which awaits him the next morning. And he is set free and enabled to die shouting praise to God.

Now here too it seems to me that the objection can be raised that an essentially magical operation is being proposed, in which the magus sets the terms of the work. Here perhaps we are at the line between Theurgy in which one makes oneself available to God for the working of his operation, and sorcery in which one on the other hand uses God as a resource for one's own operation, or, if one is a better man, one's own imaging of God's purpose. I do not know that Williams always entirely avoids the danger here (yet if to seek to do good on one's own terms be sorcery, who of us has never dabbled in the black art?) Many who live by faith no doubt are, or appear to be, near this line, from the 'faith missionary' acting on the assumption that God will move people to give to sustain the work he has begun in God's name, to Peter who provides in his word to the lame man in the temple gate "In the Name of Jesus, rise..." the perfect example of Theurgy, which is yet, externally viewed, not so different from an operation of presumption or of sorcery. Charles Williams was both Christian and Mage. He attempted in writing to express the inexpressible. But perhaps he was the more exceptional in attempting in his life to work the Apostolic Theurgy, the Mystery of the word of power spoken from the ground of substituted love.

At the same time, beyond the assumption of burdens through a transaction on an inner and mystical plane, we have always the possibility of making exchanges or substitutions on a practical level. For example, if someone lacks the sort of mind which can cope with filling out tax-returns, and I have that ability and offer to do it for him, that is also a real substitution which, as done for and within the love of God, will also effect a spiritual transaction. Perhaps for many, alertness to such possibilities of service, and taken seriously this involves a discipline of attention to those given to us (as C.S. Lewis says, surely after the Blessed Sacrament, our neighbor is the holiest thing in our daily world), will be the most natural way to exercise the transaction of that exchange which, as Williams says, is the pattern of the Kingdom.

Besides the overtly miraculous exchange, and the exchange which appears simply practical and yet contains the miracle of substituted love, there is another more subtle experience of exchange, in which our modest and simple offering of service is met and completed by the miraculous.

So I have a letter from Manyasha, a young student of theatre and aspiring actress who also studies at the Youth Missionary School, which our community sponsors in Moscow. She tells of the trip of a group from the School to do a program for the Christmas season at a juvenile prison in Ardatov, a small city several hundred miles east of Moscow. The boys confined there are not, when they come in, the hardest cases. Indeed many have sentences of some years for what amount to misdemeanors (one boy they spoke to was in for three years for walking a rich man's dog without permission, just on a whim and with no reasonably chargeable intention of stealing the dog). Yet the life is hard and many come back from such places hardened themselves and with ice in their hearts. Manyasha writes:

> We did not know what to expect, and we had no special program and only a guitar and the willingness to share. We met with the first program, about 80 boys from 12 to 18 showed up in their short

black uniforms...They stood to greet us and then sat down. We decided to share our testimonies with them, to tell them about when and how we came to know the Lord. We sang, read poetry. Andrey talked about Christmas and how God who was incarnate had a love for all of Creation...Very unexpectedly to me, a trusting and silent atmosphere was achieved. The boys first became serious and then, the cruel expressions on faces faded away and we were smiling at each other! How did it happen, this miracle that in our first visit, God's presence was felt so strongly...and it was so clear and accepted that God is the only one these boys were longing for? As we spoke for that short time, they became very open and sincere, and shared with us their spiritual wounds, their life catastrophes, their pain of abandonment.

You know it may be there is a time in every person's life of special encounter with God and of feeling his presence. The time we from the School had in the Ardatov prison was such a time for us I think. We felt the Saviour's fulfilled 'Give and you shall receive!' Fulfilled, and that we had learned something about ourselves.

How we desire that our weaknesses may always be a door for Jesus!!!

Now it seems to me that there was an Exchange here. We may say that the young people from the School set aside their uncertainty, going cold into such a strange and unpredictable environment, and the boys of the prison in turn set aside their defenses, and each shared their stories, of loss and of consolation, and all gained. It was a kind of Christmas miracle, each bringing what he had to the presence of the Eternal Childhood of God. White magic indeed in a place Manyasha describes as 'lost in the white of snow and of low clouds...'

Peter, a young Japanologist, considers the trip to Ardatov and asks himself first why he needed to go, and then why the prisoners there needed that visit, and "why we, as a little community, needed this trip."

He says that for him it was a test of himself in a new situation, more deeply a test of his sincerity and of his willingness to meet God by facing others in their need. For the young men in the prison it was really the same, turned around: the opportunity to face 'another life and other values and to meet God in this, finding that *we are important* to God and to other people...' For the Community the pattern of exchange is the Same: 'we experience trust of God and of each other, and give witness from these relationships. Finally we learn together that we have only what we have given, and then...Christ is among us!'

White magic, the magi, 'lost in the white of the snow and the clouds.'

This also is community...the continual exchanges... of forgiveness...of prayer. Lord, your peace and love, through my offered emptiness, to the brothers and sisters and (only) then finally it is mine...my sorrows and happinesses to theirs, to turn (only in your way, Lord) all to final joy. My life to the way of exchange. All for All. Amen.

19

REVELATION

THE BOOK OF REVELATION IS THE most Liturgical in the
Bible. It starts with a blessing to the lector who will
read it to the assembly. Its narration moves from and
ever returns to the chants of the Liturgy above. It
again and again identifies that Liturgy with the Eucharist, heavenly and earthly, by its imagery.

This has consequences which go beyond the merely
liturgical and touch the height and depth of our vision
of the world, and are worth some little meditation. But
perhaps first in that meditation we ought to establish a little
more in what way the book shows its liturgical character.

It is given 'on the Lord's day,' the day of the
Liturgy, and it is announced,

> Blessed is he that readeth and they that hear.

Then there are all the references which in early Christian symbolism clearly represent the Eucharist; the
eating from the Tree of Life (2:17), the hidden manna
(2:24), the statement that 'the Lamb shall feed them'
(7:17), and the exultant,

> Blessed are they which are called to the Marriage
> Supper of the Lamb (19:9).

—to point up a few.

Beyond this, and perhaps still deeper in the fabric of this vision, there are the hymns, of which there are at least eight, from the 'Holy, Holy, Holy...' (4:8-11) to the re-echoing at the end (22:21) of the four-fold Maranatha, 'Come!..Come!..Come!..Come!..' of the Beasts in chapter six.

An approach to another level of this Celestial Liturgy was attempted by Austin Farrer of Oxford in his *Rebirth of Images* in which he argued that the cycle of Biblical festival worship, and of the seasons and of the patterns of the stars, underlay the whole. So the lampstands signal the Feast of Dedication, the censers, elders and Lamb show the time of Passover, the trumpets announce the New Year and so on. I do not think this ingenious theory was ever refuted, or even opposed head-on, but Farrer in a later work, perhaps feeling he had gone too far with it, backed off in writing a conventional commentary for Oxford University Press. Indeed it is only too easy to find and then impose and extend patterns, yet perhaps the truth of Farrer's early work lies less in the reliance of revelation on Jewish festival worship than in that larger reality which is represented, that it draws in the whole cycle of the universe and of the earth, of our days and of eternity. That, in effect, images drawn from the pattern of worship and calendar here are recombined and used creatively, not simply as a sort of literary reference (like the pattern of the Odyssey in James Joyce's *Ulysses* which serves to suggest depth and resonance) but to make present something other and higher. In any case, *Rebirth of Images* must rank among the most wonder-charged pieces of Biblical scholarship of our time.

Now, whatever else it may be, *Revelation* is surely among the greatest of poems (as Farrer says, the greatest Christian poem, purely on literary ground, before Dante). But what book of comparable literary weight is read so perversely?

Everyone would agree that to read Dante's *Inferno* as a tour of Hell (and not first of all as an inner journey) would be wrong. Yet even today many read the *Book of Revelation* as if it were something like Nostradamus' prophecies. We suggest that of course the Revelation relates to the struggle of the early Church and the Roman Empire (as Biblical Prophecy, as Isaiah for example in his time), and that beyond that it echoes the whole of history (as an apocalypse like Daniel), but that it is not a fortune-teller's book. Also, that its deep and unique core, saving it from the mere seminary categories of prophecy and apocalypse, is worship.

Yet it is little used in Christian worship either as matter for reading (indeed it is not, partly due to the date of composition of the canon, read in the Eastern Church at all) or, more importantly, as pattern and model of Liturgy.

It may be that this reflects a certain 'crisis of imagination' in the Church today. Visual imagination and deep feeling tend to be left to art, music and poetry...while theology lays claim now only reason and clarity. Perhaps Eastern theology claims to be whole, and it is from this rejection of the division of reason and mysticism that Vladimir Lossky begins his important *Mystical Theology of the Eastern Church*, and perhaps indeed it has useful possibilities of expressing wholeness, but it seems to me that this wholeness is more often praised than manifested and the crisis is no less with us of the Eastern Church.

There seems to be a paradoxical and terrible limitation to our experience of worship, that loss of the Cosmic dimension goes hand in hand with a separation from ordinary daily life. So a Liturgy takes place in a space which is neither our world nor the Eden above, but an artificial space as separated from the reality below as from that above. It is this which Fr. Venaimin Nowack of St. Petersberg has made the central concern of his, unfortunately largely unpublished, work in the field of political science. Fr. Veniamin found that Russian Orthodox piety typically presents the faithful with the black-and-white alternatives of an imagined heaven or hell, and yet little guidance as to how to live in the world as we experience it, this 'middle-earth.' What he suggests as ground within the Eastern tradition for the pluralism which democracy requires, is the way of 'negative theology' with its emphasis on the limits of our knowledge, and therefore the need to leave space for multiple interpretations. This deepening of our vision to its limits, is precisely what a cosmic (rather than a rite-centered) vision of Liturgy offers. Of course the specific implications of the absence of this cosmic dimension ,will vary from culture to culture. So the affluent societies, while pluralistic, are left with that deadening banality which results from a pluralism not grounded in the sense of the Divine world's presence.

Now, the larger and cosmic vision of the Liturgy once was an accepted understanding in the Church. So St. Maximus begins his *Mystagogy* (introduction to Liturgy)with the discussion of how the Church, the human body, and the universe are alike as being places of Liturgy. So the inner Liturgy of the heart, and the Liturgy of the gathered Church, and the Liturgy of the Universe itself, all reflect each other, and, each inseparable from the others, they form finally a single Liturgy. This was replaced for most eastern Christians by the allegorical interpretations of Nicholas Cabasilas (for whom the acolyte bearing a candle at vespers is John the Baptist and so on,) or, more recently, by the 'liturgical movement' understanding of Liturgy as 'the work of the people of God,' which is good as far as it goes, but somehow lacking in cosmic and inner depth, a lack reflective, as it may be, of our crisis of imagination.

In Revelation everything is brought together. The contemporary Greek theologian Agoridis says:

> For John, liturgy, prayer, God, heaven and all the terrifying things happening here on earth are not unrelated...they form a unity, they are one thing.

He adds:

> The Liturgy in Revelation shows the true meaning of history as opposed to the falseness which seems to dominate its visible direction the transition from the one period of the world (the false history to the other (its inner truth) is presented as extremely painful.

If our Liturgy tends to drift towards an inauthentic place touching neither earth nor heaven, then perhaps Revelation is, as Petros Vasiliadis, another contemporary Greek teacher, says,

> the key to the discovery of the real meaning of Christian worship...

However is not Revelation, like Dante's great *Comedia*, also an inner journey on one important level? With Dante it is obvious: he is lost in a forest 'in the middle of life's way' and the only way out is through his inner darkness to the mountain of Purgatory and, past all his false personality which holds him there,to its summit and beyond on the road that leads among the stars...

Can we see this level in the *Book of Revelation?* I should say absolutely yes...although as a less central and conscious intention of the author.

The English poet Christina Rossetti, who spent her last seven years studying *Revelation,* said:

> Whatever the Beast of Revelation may be in history...it is also like that world, flesh and devil which are my daily antagonists and of which I must daily, hourly, momentarily, beware.

There are things in our heart which, as they come to the surface, appear as dark as the Beast or as false as the Whore of Babylon. These things also must be faced...within the light of Christ and with the courage and honesty which only complete reliance on God and humility can provide. They are terrible, threatening things...but also their reality is so much less than God's that, overcome, they may seem but the masks of mummers at Carnival and 'like as smoke vanishes...or as wax melts before the fire.'

And then the New Jerusalem appears. It is a cube in form with 1,000 miles to each side...but the cube represents the whole of space (as for example marked out in blazing lines in the Jewish *Sepher Yetzirah,* Book of Creation). There is now no sun and moon and the sea is gone, but surely nothing is lost and all is transformed and included within that cubic city of the renewed or realized Cosmos. And so also we, or 'He who overcomes'(REV.3:12), begin to experience now, fulfilling the Master's word that 'The Kingdom of God is within you.'

Just as the inner Liturgy reflects the outer...so our inner combat with evil is reflected in history and in the Cosmos. One participates in Cosmic redemption by individual ascetic effort, against inner evil and, on the other hand, by one's worship in the heart and in the community.

So the Revelation invites us at once towards heaven and at the same time towards seeing and overcoming evil and our inner darkness, and it is a single invitation. In this the words of wise Heraclitus are fulfilled that 'the way up and the way down are one.' And in this we understand why those who meditated on the ascent of Elijah by flaming chariot were called 'those who go down to the chariot.' How desperately we need both these things...the vision of the Glory and the dispelling of the heart's darkness. More than that, how our heart longs to join in the worship of the whole Cosmos—and what joy when we feel our word enter that ever sounding word of praise which is the fiery heart of all things!

At that moment we find that the Revelation is fulfilled not simply at the end of history, but at every moment of history. Its beginning and end are already and here and now. Its story is the inner truth of my life today.

So while it may be wonderful to restore the Book of Revelation to the public reading it supposes—

Blessed is he who reads and those who hear,

what is prior is for those who lead worship, and for

each person, for you and I, to recover that deep sense of worship as a whole, a whole which is visual, musical, of the heart and of history, of our day and of every day and of Eternity. This sense of worship is recoverable in the heart, and in the Community, the Church, and where it is recovered there is and shall be (may it be so!) fire and living water and the Church itself, indeed the Cosmos itself, seen new in Christ.

Let it be so speedily and in our time!

Amen. Even so Come Lord Jesus!

20

HEAVEN

A REPORTER INTERVIEWED A HASSIDIC TEACHER who was noted as a master of Jewish spiritual tradition, and after many questions finally asked one which seemed impossible to answer because it referred to a work of immense length and complexity which stands at the very heart of that tradition…"Ravi, can you give in a word the meaning of the *Book of Splendour* (Sepher ha Zohar)?" Immediately he replied:

"That what is above is the same as what is below."

•

It is said that a man named Balinas entered a cave and found there a king robed in red seated on a throne whom Balinas somehow, as if in a dream, knew to be Hermes, the thrice-blessed, legendary ruler of Egypt. And in the King's hand was a great emerald on which, as on a tablet, were inscribed words…in an elder language, Syriac, beginning:

> True, it is, without falsehood, certain and most true
> [*Verum*, in another elder tongue with the sound of
> sacred incantation, *sine mendacio, certum et*

verissimum] that which is above is like to that which is below and that which is below is like to that which is above *[et quod est inferius est sicut id quod est superius]* to accomplish the miracles of the One!

From an ancient cave and the words etched on living stone or from whatever other source, these words echo, and their resonance fills the Renaissance where Hermes stands beside Moses as his teacher on the pavement of Siena...

As above, so below... The ancient idea lives still, and even in the modern childrens' books about Mary Poppins by Pamela Travers:

> The Park Keeper took his mother's arm...darkness filled the sky like a tide, [leaving] only two points of light. "That there star," he said, pointing, "and the night light on the porch, if you look at them long enough...you can hardly tell which is which!" [His mother] smiled at him comfortably.
> "Well, one's the shadow of the other."

True perhaps in a fairy tale, but the lights in the sky we know seem so remote from our little lights...

•

Now it is Midnight of Easter. The church empties at the tolling of the bells and the faithful bearing candles form a circle of moving flame as they circuit it, through the night to the discovery of the empty tomb, all the while singing:

> The angels in heaven *(quod est superius)*
> Sing thy Resurrection O Christ!
> Make us *(quod est inferius)* on earth worthy also...

Hermes' word written not in emerald but in a circle of living flame, a circle in the night beneath the circle of lights of Deep Heaven which joins the circle below. Or have we risen into it? This is a sky no longer distant... not the sky we know.

Hermes' word is fulfilled in Resurrection... and Resurrection is as good a word as we have for Heaven, is it not? What is Heaven if not the Resurrected life of all things in Christ?

Now, in seeing Heaven, seeing the Resurrection, through the lens of the first hymn of the Paschal night and beyond that of the Emerald tablet, we are not suggesting that this world we know is Heaven. Not at all. Only in its Resurrection...

So the theology which emphasizes that God is ever beyond and 'wholly other,' transcendent, can be true... It is true as descriptive of the un-Resurrected world... And the speech about God which emphasizes that he is present and inward to the world, is absolutely right, but only if it is a theology of Resurrection.

It is Resurrection which makes Hermes' word true...which makes above and below true reflections of each other...On the other hand if the Resurrection fulfills the ancient word, as it does all true words, the Emerald Tablet (when it is illumined by that Resurrection light) provides a way of thinking of, and a glass for seeing towards, Heaven.

According to a very old text, parallel to the Bible and from the heart of the early Church, the disciples asked Jesus how they could become as little children and enter the Kingdom of Heaven, and the Master replied:

> You will enter when you make the inner as the outer, and the lower as the upper...

'Marcel,' narrator of *Remembrance of Things Past*, the great novel of Marcel Proust, says

> And at that moment when recovering my balance I put my foot on a stone which was slightly lower than its neighbors, all my discouragement vanished. In its place was that same happiness which at various epochs of my life had been given to me...a profound azure intoxicated my eyes, impressions of coolness, of dazzling light.

He calls these moments 'Resurrections'—moments of breaking free and recovering the integrity of the self beyond the fragmentation caused by passing time...In that moment inner world and outer...upper world and lower, past and future, are at Peace. Heaven. Every moment that was or is or shall be can be Resurrected... without missing one... The Good Shepherd is able to find it. Heaven leaves nothing untouched, leaves nothing behind, leaves nothing in the tomb.

> *Ad perpetranda miracula rei Unius.*
> —To accomplish the miracles of the One.

Gray sky...suddenly the azure sky of Wisdom! The city with its gray pavement becomes in a rush that infinite cubic City of Revelation—one thousand miles to an edge, traced, the *Book of Creation* says, by the Most High's ten words of lightning which reach to the end of the universe: 'And they widen and continue to eternity,' that curious old book adds, apparently suggesting the cosmic cube as an expanding universe ... In any case it is only in that transformation, and only then, not before then, that the world is what it will be and so already is and remains.

Mihail, a young chemist and member of Hosanna in Moscow, writes of such an experience:

> It was not a vision, nor an ecstatic experience, but a thought which came and touched me deeply while I was riding as usual on the metro and afterwards even entered a dream... I arrive at the subway station and realize that it is no longer a station within my usual life. The station is filled with light, the pillars are of a kind of precious stone, like emerald or sapphire, and I have the feeling of returning home from a very long journey. I hear the train conductor say in a voice ever so gentle, "Alright! now we have arrived, it is the end." And my heart fills with joy and peace. Perhaps people who meet the second coming in the Metro will feel like that...

Usually in dreams and reveries about travel, it seems we do not arrive...the station disappears as we are changing trains and becomes a field...we become separated from our party... Trains are the most routine of things and perhaps this indicates that our routine life is..not arriving. There is no completion possible in dreams because there is no completion in our experience.

Mihail's dream is a sign of completion in this life and beyond it also... It is a Resurrection, until the moment of Resurrection is lost.

But some day it will not be lost. All the salt tears will have been shed, all that will remain then is the inner truth, which was there before and which now stands alone...One abides (I Cor. 13).

The miracles of the One are accomplished this Resurrection night, and will yet be accomplished...

> Make us on earth worthy also to worship thee with Purity of heart.

And then even now it is not lost...even for those who return from that circle of light falling into the sky beyond the sky we know...

> Two Welsh knights came back...and they were asked why they were so happy and they said to those who inquired: "Go to where we have been and you shall know the Why."

Beyond the sky we know...

21

Morning

It has been a long night, night of the
Paschal Mystery...

"Christ is Risen!"
I trace the cross in the air.
Al Nur has kept a double fast, Lent and Ramadan.

As he takes my descending hand in both of his ,
his eyes search mine for a long moment
(as of a drumbeat. OOO Allahhh...) Then,

"He is Risen in us! and for us! and with us!
and through us!"

Now Bill Draper is celebrating Holy Communion
of Easter for a group of Americans in Japan.
Tall, elderly, with a booming laugh ("my
wife says I sound like an Australian")
now as he reads the word of institution, why
is he weeping like a child?

The rebbe took one of his hassids to the window
to show him something and they both began to weep.
"What is he showing him?"
"The light of the Jerusalem which shall be."
"Then why are they crying?"
"Because he is also showing him all the pain
which the holy people of God must suffer
before that Great Day."

Now Bill raises the chalice.. of what morning
is the light which now glints from it?

22

LIGHT

EARLY IN THE YET DIM MORNING on a path at Delphi, a serpent runs ahead of the pilgrim on the ground marking a sinuous way to... There, suddenly, an ancient altar above which butterflies rise in a perfect spiral into a descending pillar of light.

Lost in the Light

Light so reminds of God. Indeed St. John tells us that "God...is...light." St. Gregory Palamas, who thought long and deeply on the mystery of light, held that there is created light, which is natural, but then there is another light which is uncreated and Divine: that light which blazed over Mount Tabor was uncreated and it is this light which those who pray may experience as an illumination of mind and heart.

Lost in the Light...

What light is this in the morning air? What if those speak true who say that visible light and the *Lumen de Lumine,* the Light of Light, be of a single spectrum, and Light be One?

Lumen de Lumine...

Here there is nothing to search or probe...nothing to be known about it...and so a forgetting pertains to the comprehension of this place. So open your eyes and see this great and awesome secret. Happy is one whose eyes shine from this secret, in this world and the world to come!

DAVID BEN JUDAH, *THE BOOK OF MIRRORS*

[There are] inaccessible insights by which the intellect is swallowed up in Wonder, forgetting...

ST. ISAAC OF SYRIA

St. Isaac speaks of Wonder, and it is a Syriac word which means 'amazement' or even a forgetting in amazement or wonder, as being integral knowledge. Now integral knowledge is a kind of Grail of modern science, the Unified Field Theory of Einstein's quest, and is the ancient quest of Adam to know God and the world and himself at the same time without needing, as we most generally do, to lay down knowledge of the one to know the other. Perhaps Wonder is the answer, and as this light we see is sign of (or it may be is of the same spectrum as) that Light of Light, so the little wonder we feel is a beginning of that Wonder which St. Isaac says is the way of knowledge of the world to come.

Lost in the Shadow, lost in the Light...

Then it is deep night and I am writing a greeting for Easter for my brothers and sisters, writing ahead of knowledge perhaps...

—CHRIST IS RISEN!

Christ is indeed Risen…do we see Him, our Lord? 'If the eye be one the whole body is full of light.'

Just yesterday with one eye, I saw the Glory of the Lord, and with the other eye I saw my own brokeness, and that of the Church, and that of the world… And then I did not understand, or see a way forward.

'If the eye is One…'

Is not the Mystery of the 'Single Eye,' of the 'Luminous Eye,' the Mystery of the Resurrection? Yesterday I saw with two eyes and two thoughts. Today I see that the Lion of Judah and the Offered Lamb are One…the Risen Lord is the One with the marks on the hands and side…and my poor life, its moments and days and turning thoughts, these also are what will be Resurrected…this body, and this life, and not another as Job saw. This Church, this family in Christ, and not another, this world itself, and not another…

Today I see with a single eye and all is full of Light…

•

And as I share this thought which only begins to be mine, in this sharing it is mine, and the world of Light is here and it is now… and here is the Gate of Wonder…

And so it is again and now today, writing passes to simplest prayer...

Lumen de Lumine Illumine us!

November 5th 1998
Feast of St Michael and All the Angelicals